M000281833

TERRIFIC
IDEAS
FOR
Gardening

500
TERRIFIC
IDEAS
FOR
Gardening

Anne Halpin

A Round Stone Press Book

A Fireside Book
Published by
SIMON & SCHUSTER INC.
NEW YORK LONDON TORONTO SYDNEY TOKYO

FIRESIDE
Simon and Schuster Building
Rockefeller Center
1230 Avenue of the Americas
New York, New York 10020

A Round Stone Press Book

Directors: Marsha Melnick, Paul Fargis, Susan E. Meyer
Design: Jeff Fitschen
Illustrations: Ray Skibinski

Fireside and colophon are registered trademarks of
    Simon & Schuster Inc.

Manufactured in the United States of America

1 2 3 4 5 6 7 8 9 10

Library of Congress Cataloging-in-Publication Data

Halpin, Anne, 1952-
    500 terrific ideas for gardening/Anne Halpin.
            p.   cm.
    "A Round Stone Press Book"
    "A Fireside Book"
    ISBN 0-671-73718-X
    1. Gardening—Miscellanea   I. Title. II. Title: Five hun-
dred terrific ideas for gardening.
SB453.H214   1993
635—dc20   92-3202
                                                      CIP

Contents

INTRODUCTION

Gardening is a most rewarding activity. We gardeners are caretakers of a little piece of the Earth, nurturing growth and life. For our effort, we are rewarded with a bounty of sensual delights: the shimmering beauty of flowers; the textures, shapes, and colors of foliage; the incomparable flavors of fresh herbs, vegetables, and fruit; the mysterious, romantic, or refreshing sensation of fragrance.

Most of all, gardening is fun. Trying something new in the garden each year helps keep it fun.

Most gardeners are great experimenters. We are always looking for a new flower to grow, a better way to water or prune, or a clever trick for producing more tomatoes. We also need help solving our garden problems: what to plant in the shade of a favorite tree, how to hide a chain-link fence, how to extend the growing season. And at all times we strive to save ourselves time and work.

This book offers a potpourri of useful ideas for many kinds of gardens, and gardening situations. There are tips on growing vegetables, annual and perennial flowers, fruits, herbs, lawns and groundcovers, and trees and shrubs. There are also suggestions that address container gardening and several kinds of specialty gardens. For each type of garden, you will find ideas for soil building, planting, propagation, pruning, fertilizing, combating pests and diseases, watering, and weeding, as well as tips on designing the garden and choosing and using tools and equipment.

The ideas in this book come from my own experience, from friends, relatives, fellow gardeners, and other experts, and from a whole host of other sources. It is my hope that gardeners of all stripes, whatever their level of expertise and no matter what kind of garden they have, will find some suggestions here to interest them and inspire them in their efforts.

1

DESIGN

1 start small

The most useful piece of advice for a new gardener is "start small." When you are just getting started in gardening, it is very easy to plant a garden that is too big to maintain. For your first garden, pick out just a few different plants—your absolute favorites—and plant them in a modest-sized bed, no larger than 4×12 feet. If you are planning a flower garden, use a simple scheme of two or three colors.

2 take the time to plan

Resist the urge to run out to the garden center on the first warm spring day and buy whatever plants strike your fancy. Take the time to plan out your garden in advance; it's well worth the effort. A well-planned garden looks better, grows better, and, where edibles are involved, produces better.

3 plan using your property survey

A garden plan should start with a map of your property. You can use graph paper to make a map, but a simpler way is to start with your property survey. Get some enlarged xeroxes of the survey, and draw in paths, walls, and other permanent features; then sketch in possible planting areas on overlay sheets of tracing paper or clear acetate. On another overlay, note sun and shade patterns over the course of a day at different times of year. This method allows you to plan for as many or as few garden elements as you choose.

4 gardens are for people

For the most comfortable landscape, keep all the elements in scale with the human body. Place focal points where they are easy to see. Plan hedges and other screening plants to be high enough so that you can't see over them. Set flagstones in a path at a comfortable stepping distance apart. Select benches that are beautiful and also a nice height for sitting.

5 keep in touch

Plant your garden as close to the house as possible, so you will pass through it often. Close contact with the garden allows you to spot problems when they first appear, before they have a chance to really take hold. It also makes it easy to pull a few weeds here and there and to pick off spent flowers without going out of your way.

6 a safe distance

If your garden is close to your house, garage or another outbuilding, and the structure is made of stucco, plaster, or cement, it may be unwise to plant closer than 2 feet from the wall. A lot of lime may have gotten into the soil during construction, creating highly alkaline conditions that are unhealthy even for plants that prefer alkaline soil. In addition to allowing for a 2-foot margin, it is also a good idea to remove the top 3 feet of soil from the bed and replace it with fresh soil.

7 match plants to conditions

The most important key to a successful garden is to match plants to available growing conditions. Even the best gardener cannot make a sun-loving plant grow in shade or a moisture-lover grow in dry soil. Choosing plants that do well in the conditions you have to offer makes gardening easier and more effective because you are working with nature instead of against it.

8 how many plants to buy

Here's a formula to use to figure out how many plants to order for a particular space in the garden: As a general rule, assume that a full-grown plant will be half to two-thirds as wide as it is tall. Most seed and nursery catalogs list plant heights, but many do not give widths.

9 plant in well-drained soil

Good drainage is essential for a healthy garden, no matter what kind of soil you have. Do not try to grow plants in a low spot where water collects after rain. Soggy soil has insufficient oxygen for plants, stays cold longer in spring, and is usually of poor fertility.

10 don't plant in a cold pocket

Do not locate garden beds at the bottom of a hill, if you can avoid it. Cold air will roll down the slope and collect at the bottom, forming a "cold pocket" where plants may be damaged by late frosts in spring and early frosts in fall.

11 tough plants for tough places

For a thriving garden near a driveway, street, or sidewalk, where plants are subject to stress from dust, fumes, and traffic, grow durable annuals like marigolds, geraniums, petunias, dusty miller, and perennials like sedums and sempervivums.

12 let the sun shine in

For maximum sun exposure, orient your garden so the rows or beds run east to west. Plant the shortest plants in the front (on the south side) of the garden and the tallest ones in the back (on the north side), where they will not cast shadows on the smaller plants.

13 minimize wind problems

If you live in a windy location, minimize the drying effect of the wind by planting downwind of your house or garage or another existing windbreak such as a fence or hedge. It also helps to align garden rows or beds at a 90-degree angle to the direction of the prevailing winds.

14 create a windbreak

If your garden is subject to frequent strong winds, you will probably need to install a windbreak. Pit it on the side of the garden from which the prevailing winds blow. A windbreak can be a row of shrubs, a hedge, or a wall or fence. Walls and fences are more effective as windbreaks when they are of open—rather than solid—construction. Wind may jump over a solid barrier, creating bizarre air patterns.

15 the importance of open space

Open spaces covered by grass, groundcovers, paving, pebbles, or even water are as important to a home garden as planted beds and borders. Without open space, plantings have less shape, and the garden can't be used for sitting, dining, or even viewing plants up close. Don't forget to plan for open spaces in your home landscape. If open space is clearly defined and in pleasing proportion to the rest of the garden, the garden design will be attractive year-round.

16 garden rooms

If the idea of designing a garden from scratch is daunting, you may find it easier to think of the garden as a room and the plants as furnishings. Like an indoor room, the garden can have walls to divide it from other parts of the yard (fences, walls, hedges, rows of shrubs, or trellised vines), a floor (grass or groundcover), and furniture (plants). Different "rooms" in the garden can contain different kinds of plants (roses, perhaps, or cutting flowers) and different color schemes.

17 a question of balance

If a formal herb garden, flower bed, or border does not look quite right, it may be because the balance is off. An ornamental garden must be designed with balance. This quality is gained by designing the garden around one or more axes—imaginary straight lines that pass through the design. Axes often take the form of paths. The most important features in a formal garden are placed along the main axis. If they are slightly off the axis, the garden will look off balance, but it may be difficult to discern why.

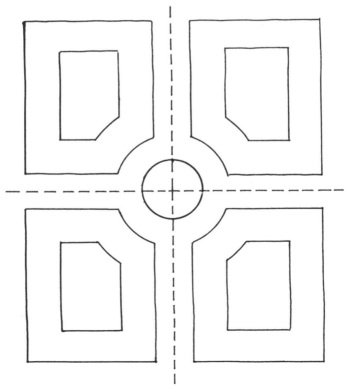

18 access in a large garden

In a large flower garden, allow narrow pathways through the garden so you can get in to weed, water, and groom the plants. Put down some mulch to keep your shoes clean. When the plants are full grown, they will hide the paths.

19 a winding path

A path, even a small one, that curves through a large garden or landscape adds a feeling of mystery and anticipation to the scene. Visitors walking along a winding path can't help but wonder what's around the corner. Unless you are designing a formal garden, make the paths curved instead of straight.

20 plotting the curve

An easy way to decide on just the right shape for a curved bed or border is to outline the design with a garden hose. Before you start to dig, lay the hose on the ground and adjust it until you find the right size and shape for a bed or the best curve for a border.

21 attaining symmetry

To get both sides of a curved border to match, first lay out one side with a garden hose and mark it with lime. Then take a length of string and measure the width you want the border to be. Mark the width on the string and measure this width at intervals to plot the curve of the other side of the border, marking the curve with lime.

22 pictorial space in a garden

Imagine your garden as a landscape painting, with the space divided into a foreground, middle ground, and background. Planning a succession of plant heights, with short plants in front and tall plants in back, creates an illusion of greater depth, much like the pictorial space in a painting. Graduating the plant heights also lets you see all the plants in the garden. In a border or bed that will be viewed from one side, place the tallest plants at the back. In an island bed that can be seen from all sides, put the tallest plants in the middle.

23 make a small garden seem bigger

To get more from a tiny yard, design the garden in a series of terraced raised beds. Terracing will enable you to fit more plants into the space than if the garden is all on one level. It also creates an illusion of more space and greater depth. Terracing is also very useful on sloped ground. It keeps soil from washing downhill.

24 tiered bed to save space

Use aluminum garden edging to create three levels in a small space. Bend one strip of edging into a 6-foot-diameter circle. Nail the cut ends to a foot-long wood stake, and nail three more stakes at regular intervals around the circle. Pound the stakes into the ground to anchor the edging. Put down a layer of coarse sand or fine gravel for drainage; then fill with light, loamy soil. Repeat the procedure to make a 4-foot ring, and set this ring in the center of the first one. Add sand and then soil. Repeat the procedure again to make a 2-foot ring.

This tiered bed is perfect for strawberries, salad plants, herbs, or annuals.

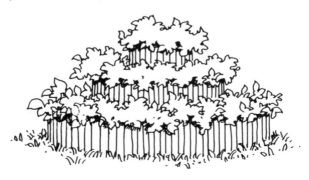

25 use terraces on a hillside

A gentle slope is a good place for a garden: The soil will drain well, and cold air will roll down the hill and collect at the bottom, bypassing the garden. But too steep a slope may be difficult to plant and maintain. If the slope drops more than 1 foot over an expanse of 50 feet, construct terraces running across the face of the hill to create garden beds.

26 the simplest terrace

If a slope is not too steep, you can create simple terraced beds by standing rows of flagstones or other flat stones on edge at intervals along the slope. Fill in each level with soil to create flat planting beds.

27 anchor ties in place

Railroad-tie terraces are a great way to turn a steep hillside into a usable garden, but when building the terraces, do not forget to include anchor ties. The anchors are set into the hill at right angles to the terrace timbers and help hold them together. Metal stakes inserted vertically through holes drilled near the ends of the ties provide further support.

28 safe wood for gardens

If you will be using railroad ties or other lumber to build raised beds or terraces, be sure the wood is treated with a preservative that is nontoxic to plants. Never use railroad ties that have been soaked in creosote. Zinc naphthenate and copper naphthenate are both considered safe. Of the two, copper naphthenate is a better preservative, but its unearthly green color will take a year or so to fade to a more natural hue.

29 illusions with color

In the garden, as in painting, cool colors seem to recede and warm colors appear to come forward. To make a small garden appear bigger and more spacious, plant flowers in cool, light colors. To make a large, sprawling garden feel more intimate, choose bright, warm colors.

30 light up a shady spot

To brighten and lighten a shady corner of the garden, plant white or light pastel flowers, such as white or pink impatiens, wax begonias, astilbe, azaleas, or rhododendrons, to make the garden glow. Sweet pepper bush (*Clethra alnifolia*) bears fragrant white blossoms that perfume a shady garden in late summer.

31 scaling plants to beds

How tall should the tallest plants in an island bed be? Choose plants whose mature height is equal to about half the width of the bed. Place these plants in the center of the bed so they can be viewed from all sides.

32 fake sunlight

To create an illusion of dappled sunlight in a shady spot, plant a blend of all-green and variegated ivies, hostas, or other shade-tolerant plants.

33 trying out colors

If you are starting a new garden and are unsure of the color scheme you want, experiment by planting annuals in various shades for the first year or two. When you find a color combination you like, you can design a more permanent garden that includes perennials, shrubs, and bulbs in these colors, as well as some annuals.

34 match indoor and outdoor colors

If you want to grow flowers to cut and bring indoors, choose colors that will go with the decor of your home, as well as colors that will harmonize with one another in the garden.

35 color scheme shortcut

One way to create a harmonious mixture of colors in a flower garden is to plant varieties of one type of flower. Want an example? Think about pink, rose, lavender, and purple petunias, or nasturtiums in shades of mahogany, red, orange, and gold. Different-colored varieties of the same flower species, or members of the same hybrid series, almost always harmonize with one another.

36 color combinations

Some harmonious or analogous color combinations for flower gardens are red, rose, and pink; pink, blue, and purple; and red, orange, and yellow. Complementary or contrasting colors are pink and yellow, purple and yellow, blue and orange, or blue, violet, and yellow. Or try red and white, or blue and white for a more formal feeling.

37 blender colors

A good trick for harmonizing colors that might otherwise be jarring is to include blender colors in the garden. Drifts or clumps of white or pale yellow flowers soften groups of stronger colors. Silver foliage is an effective harmonizer for bright pinks and strong blues, and it looks lovely with softer pinks, blues, and lavender. Dark green leaves help to tone down bright, hot reds and oranges.

38 how to use bright colors

Flower gardens built on a scheme of contrasting colors can be unpleasantly jarring if not handled carefully. To make a contrasting color scheme work, choose a light, soft shade of the brightest color, or use the brightest color sparingly, as an accent, and spread the less intense colors over a larger area for balance.

39 accent with red

For an eye-stopping focal point, plant a clump of brilliant red flowers. Bright red can be overwhelming in large amounts, but it makes a stunning accent, especially beside white flowers and deep green foliage.

40 form is important

If you want to combine annuals and perennials in a flower garden, choose plant forms that complement each other. Look for annuals with growing habits that are hard to find in perennials. For example, many summer perennials have round, daisylike shapes; asters, mums, coreopsis, gaillardia, rudbeckia, and helianthus are some of the most popular summer daisy flowers. Vertical, spiky shapes are not as abundant, and some flowers that have them—such as delphiniums—can be difficult to grow. To complement round perennials, you might choose spiky annuals such as salvia or gladiolus.

41 a graceful design for flowers

In a flower garden, plan to have a gradation of plant heights from the front of the garden to the back, but let a few plants drift over the boundaries of their groups to create a softer, more integrated look.

42 a small flower garden

The easiest way to design a small flower garden is to choose three different plants and plant two or three groups of each. Repeating plants creates a harmonious, well-coordinated look, even though the design is quite simple. Here's one example: Rosy pink hybrid columbine, pale pink hardy geranium, and lavender phlox make a lovely grouping of spring perennials in a small garden.

43 group flowers for impact

Whatever kind of color scheme you choose for your flower garden, plant the flowers in groups for the best effect. Lots of single plants get lost in the design and make the garden look chaotic and spotty, like a collection of polka dots.

44 plant flowers in drifts

Colors are used most effectively in flower gardens when the flowers are planted in flowing drifts instead of straight rows like those in a traditional vegetable garden. Instead of lining up flowers like little soldiers, plant them in fluid, curved blocks. Allow the drifts to melt into each other along the edges by planting a few flowers over the boundary into the adjoining drift. Planting in drifts creates a soft, naturalistic effect.

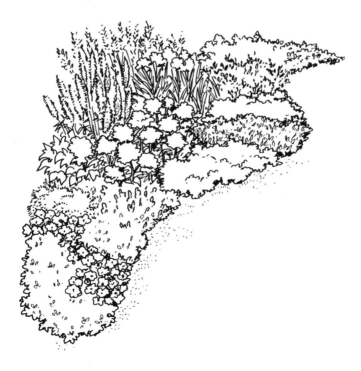

45 overplant to save space

To grow flowers with different blooming times in the same patch of ground, use a technique known as overplanting. First, plant bulbs that bloom in early spring, such as crocuses, daffodils, and tulips. Then plant shallow-rooted perennials or annuals on top of the bulbs. The bulbs will finish blooming before the other plants need the growing space.

46 timesavers

If you have little time to spend in your flower garden, grow low-maintenance plants such as impatiens, begonias, daylilies, butterfly weed, rudbeckias, and salvia. These plants are easy to grow and do not need frequent deadheading, watering, fertilizing, or other fussing in order to thrive.

47 cottage garden flowers

Cottage gardens are typified by a riot of plants—annuals, perennials, bulbs, herbs—growing together in an enclosed space. Old-fashioned varieties are more appropriate than new hybrids in such cheerful jumbles. Annuals and perennials for cottage gardens include garden pinks, sweet peas, hollyhocks, delphiniums, peonies, pansies, Johnny-jump-ups, heliotrope, larkspur, old roses, nicotiana, oriental poppies, scented geraniums, lavender, English daisies, primroses, lady's mantle, foxglove, and beebalm.

48 a hedge of peonies

Peonies have gorgeous flowers that are good for cutting and foliage that remains attractive throughout the growing season. They are easy to grow and long-lived, and they seldom need division or other maintenance. Try planting herbaceous peonies as a low hedge along a walk or driveway.

49 easy-care flowers

If you love flowers but want a garden that doesn't require a lot of maintenance, plant flowering shrubs and bulbs instead of the more labor-intensive perennials and annuals. Choose an informal design rather than a formal one that requires immaculate weeding and frequent pruning to retain its controlled appearance.

50 carefree color with bulbs

Once planted, bulbs—especially hardy bulbs—require little maintenance. Here are bulbs to plant for three seasons of almost carefree color, in order of bloom:

- In the spring—plant species crocus, snowdrop, winter aconite, anemone, glory-of-the-snow, Dutch hybrid crocus, erythronium, bulbous iris, scilla, daffodil, narcissus, and tulip.
- In the summer—plant lily, tuberous begonia, caladium, calla lily, magic lily.
- In the autumn—plant colchicum, autumn crocus, hardy cyclamen.

51 bulbs under trees

Most of our favorite spring bulbs like lots of sun. But you can still plant crocuses and daffodils under trees if the trees are deciduous. In spring, before the trees leaf out, the bulbs will get plenty of sun. Later on, they will be protected from the summer heat by the shade beneath the leafy canopy.

52 natural-looking bulbs

Whether you are planting a lot of bulbs or just a few, group them in odd numbers for a more natural, less contrived look. Groups of five, seven, or nine look more informal than groups of two, four, or six. To achieve a natural look with small bulbs, scatter them in handfuls over the soil and plant them where they fall.

53 bulbs in the lawn

If you want to naturalize bulbs in a lawn, remember that you will not be able to mow that part of the lawn in spring until the bulb foliage ripens—six to eight weeks after the flowers finish blooming. Plant the bulbs in an out-of-the-way spot, or along the edge of the main lawn.

54 bulbs for cottage gardens

Some bulbs that go especially well in a cottage garden are Madonna lily, tiger lily, snowdrop, species crocuses and tulips, poet's or pheasant's eye narcissus, crown imperial, grape hyacinth, and tuberose.

55 fall-blooming flowers

If you choose plants carefully, your flower garden can bloom well into fall. In addition to the ubiquitous chrysanthemums, consider growing hardy asters, Japanese anemone, boltonia, colchicums, lycoris, and *Sedum* 'Autumn Joy' for late-season bloom. Monkshood also flowers into autumn, and dahlias reach their peak in early fall. *Salvia* 'Victoria', marigolds, sweet alyssum, and numerous other annuals will bloom into fall if they are deadheaded or sheared back.

56 winter interest

Although the outdoor growing season ends in most gardens in fall, a well-planned landscape can be attractive in winter as well. Plant trees and shrubs with unusual branch patterns, such as the contorted hazel, also known as Harry Lauder's walking stick, or those with colorful bark, such as the red-osier dogwood. Ornamental grasses can be left standing in winter and cut back in early spring instead. Hollies and other broad-leaved evergreens and conifers also contribute color to a winter landscape.

57the easiest vines

The most adaptable, easy-to-grow vines include trumpet creeper, silver fleece vine, honeysuckle (some of which can be invasive), morning glory, moonflower, American bittersweet, Boston ivy, English ivy (which can also be invasive if not controlled), and euonymus or winter creeper.

58camouflage tactics

The easiest, most inexpensive way to hide a structure, object, or view that is less than appealing is to set up a trellis and camouflage whatever is unsightly with vines. For a change from the familiar morning glory, clematis, or wisteria, consider silver fleece vine, which bears massses of little white blossoms in autumn, Dutchman's pipe, with its rich green leaves and strangely shaped flowers, trumpet creeper, climbing hydrangea, the fragrant, night-blooming moonflower, hops (especially handsome trained on a wooden tripod), or everblooming honeysuckle. Avoid Hall's or Japanese honeysuckle, which is very invasive.

59a vine-covered bower

An excellent way to create a shady retreat in your garden is to plant Dutchman's pipe or grape vines and train them to cover an arbor. Both vines have large leaves that provide a cool canopy to block out the hot summer sun.

60vine covers

Vines that twine are perfect for covering lattice, a chain-link fence, or a downspout. Actinidia, akebia, Dutchman's pipe, bittersweet, Carolina jessamine, honeysuckle, morning glory, silver fleece vine, and wisteria are all twiners that do not need to be fastened to their support.

61 vines for warm climates

Brilliant bougainvillea seems ubiquitous in warm climates. Alternatives to consider for growing on walls, trellises, and arbors are kangaroo vine and other species of *Cissus*, orchid trumpet vine, fragrant Carolina jessamine, and stephanotis, and mandevilla with its large, exotic blossoms.

62 vines in trees

Vines climbing up into tall trees can create a lovely effect, but you must choose the vines carefully. Never plant a twining vine to climb a tree; it could strangle the tree's branches and even the trunk. A clinging vine such as climbing hydrangea is a better choice.

63 bittersweet and honeysuckle

Bittersweet and honeysuckle are delightful vines; bittersweet offers colorful berries in fall, and honeysuckle bears sweetly fragrant flowers in summer. But if you plant the wrong species, they can take over the garden. Opt for the native American species *C. scandens* instead of the invasive oriental species *C. orbiculatus*. Avoid Japanese or Hall's honeysuckle in favor of Dutch, trumpet, everblooming, or goldflame honeysuckles.

64 a portable screen

For movable shade on a patio, start with a long, rectangular planter box mounted on casters. Install a piece of lattice or some grow netting on one side of the planter and grow ivy, honeysuckle, Dutchman's pipe, or another climber to cover it. The vines will create a natural leafy screen, a quick and easy source of shade or privacy.

65 best planting pattern for vegetables

The most efficient way to use space in a bed of edibles is to set plants equidistant from one another in all directions, or in a staggered-row diagonal pattern, which allows room for more plants than a single-row garden.

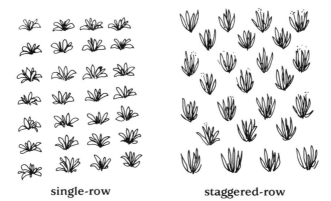

single-row   **staggered-row**

66 how high to raise a bed

If you will be making a garden in raised beds, plan on making the beds at least 6 inches higher than the surface of the surrounding soil; 1 foot is even better. If the bed is only a couple of inches high, you will not get the benefit of improved drainage that a raised bed provides.

67 the optimum width for beds

A garden bed not more than about 4 feet wide will allow you to reach the middle of the bed from both sides to weed and work around the plants. If the bed is accessible from only one side (e.g., if it is next to a fence or wall, or you have a trellis in the back of the bed), make it only as wide as you can comfortably reach. If you can reach into all parts of the bed, you will not need to walk through it and risk compacting the soil or damaging new growth.

68 the best shade for a garden

If you have old shade trees on your property that you want to keep, and if no matter where you put plants they will get some shade, plant where the tree canopy is highest and least dense. Avoid Norway and sugar maples and European beech; these trees cast deep shade. Look for trees whose lowest branches are higher than those of other trees. Do not plant the garden within a tree's dripline, the area directly below its canopy of branches.

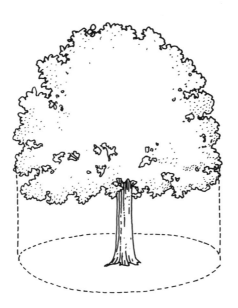

69 keeping a safe distance

Do not plant flowers or vegetables near Norway maple or black walnut trees. Keep the garden 80 to 100 feet from such trees, or at least outside their dripline. Maples have ambitious roots that travel far underground and will steal water and nutrients from garden plants. Black walnut roots contain juglone, a substance that is toxic to many other plants; it can actually poison a garden.

70 trees as protection

In climates where winter weather is severe, tall coniferous evergreens with high branches can offer some protection to sensitive shrubs, such as azaleas and rhododendrons, planted under the canopy. In such climates, deciduous trees that hold their leaves a long time in fall also protect mums and other autumn bloomers from the first light frosts, extending their blooming period.

71 lightening up shade

Even shade-tolerant plants do not grow well in dense shade. To lighten the shade in a shady garden, prune the trees high, removing some of the lower branches to allow more light to reach plants below.

72 good news about shade

Shady gardens generally need less care than gardens in full sun. There are fewer weeds and fewer pests, and plants need to be watered less often. If you have little time for gardening, plant in a shady part of your property rather than in sunny areas.

73 how much shade for shrubs?

Most broad-leaved evergreens tolerate—or even prefer—some shade. As a general rule of thumb, the shrubs with the biggest leaves can stand the most shade. For flowers, plant azaleas, rhododendrons, mountain laurel, pieris, abelia, mahonia, and, in mild climates, camellia. Hollies and barberries have colorful berries and handsome foliage.

74 a miniature water garden

If you long to grow water plants but don't have the space for a full-size pond, plant miniature varieties in a tub. Use a plastic washtub or line a wooden barrel with heavy plastic so it holds water. The tub will hold a couple of miniature water lilies, and perhaps a water fern, water snowflake, arrowhead, or other small aquatic plant.

75 romp in a meadow

Where local ordinances (and neighbors) permit, a meadow of grasses and wildflowers suited to your climate is a low-maintenance landscape with a free and easy feeling. With the right plants, you can establish a meadow in almost any kind of soil, but don't try it unless the spot gets at least six hours of direct sunlight a day.

76 keeping a meadow in place

To keep a meadow or wild garden from spreading into an adjoining lawn, plant a border of goldenrod along the edge. The goldenrod's strong root system will keep the meadow plants at bay.

77 a garden to enjoy at night

If you work all day, you can get special pleasure from your flower garden by designing it to be at its best in the evening. Grow flowers that are white, pale pink, yellow, or creamy; these light colors take on a special glow at dusk, as the colors of brighter flowers fade with the dying light. Install subtle lighting and a comfortable bench to get the maximum enjoyment from your garden at night.

78 fragrance at night

The best time to enjoy many fragrant plants is after sunset. Some scented flowers, like the lovely moonflower (*Ipomoea alba*), open their large blossoms in the afternoon and stay open all night. Many flowers, such as nicotiana, evening-scented stocks, and *Gladiolus tristis*, become fragrant, or more intensely fragrant, at night to attract nocturnal pollinators.

79 flowers birds love

Plant some of these flowers in your garden to attract birds: asters, bachelor's button, calendula, California poppy, campanula, coneflower, cosmos, marigold, garden phlox, sunflower, verbena, and zinnia. Don't plant lots of red flowers; many birds (except for hummingbirds), bees, and butterflies tend to avoid them.

80 flowers for hummingbirds

To lure hummingbirds into your garden, plant scarlet and orange varieties of American columbine, beebalm, butterfly weed, cardinal flower, fuchsia, rose of Sharon, hollyhock, jewelweed, tiger lily, trumpet vine, pineapple sage, and Indian paintbrush.

81 rock garden flowers

A few excellent flowers for rock gardens are moss pinks; basket-of-gold; small species of campanula; perennial candytuft; fringed bleeding heart; sedums, sempervivums, and other succulents; and snowdrops, miniature daffodils, and other small bulbs. All these plants are compact and easy to grow and will appreciate the well-drained soil found in a rock garden environment.

82 plants for sunny, wet places

A soggy, poorly drained spot does not have to look like a swamp. If the location gets sun or very light shade, plant Japanese primrose, marsh marigold, sweet flag, rose mallow, dogtooth violet, wood anemones, rubrum and Turk's cap lilies, globeflower, and cinnamon, royal, or ostrich ferns.

83 salt-tolerant plants

Salt can create serious problems for plants, whether it comes from ocean spray or winter roadways. Some plants that can tolerate salt are Scotch broom, big-leaf hydrangea, shore juniper, rugosa rose, and yucca.

84 plants for paths

To soften the appearance of stone steps or a flagstone path, plant mosses, Corsican mint, or creeping thyme between the stones.

85 plants for dry shade

Arguably the most difficult environment for plants is dry shade, which occurs around woody plants with shallow roots. Some plants that will grow in dry shade are lily of the valley, bleeding heart, Solomon's seal, goosneck loosestrife, ajuga, pachysandra, and goutweed (*Aegopodium*).

2

SOIL

86 how to site a new garden

When you move into a new house and are looking for the best places to plant, spots where a garden existed before are a good bet. If no garden is visible, look for wild plantain, purslane, and lamb's quarters; these weeds tend to grow in soil that has been previously cultivated.

87 gauging soil texture

No soil test will tell you much about the texture of your soil, but indicator plants can help. If mosses, sedges, curly dock, horsetail, mayapple, or joe-pye weed grow wild on your property, the soil is poorly drained. Humusy, well-drained soil is often indicated by burdock, chicory, pigweed, purslane, dandelion, and lamb's quarters. Soil that is heavy but not necessarily poorly drained may be colonized by buttercups, broad-leaved dock, dandelion, and plantain. Sandy, light soil is often home to sheep sorrel, wild cornflower, white campion, and yellow toadflax.

88 a workability test

To tell whether your soil is ready to work in spring, scoop up a handful of dirt and squeeze it into a ball with one hand; then open your fingers. If the soil ball sticks together, the soil is still too wet to work. If the ball crumbles when you release your fingers, the soil is ready for digging.

89 the best time to till

The best time to dig or till your soil is when it is just moist, neither dry nor very wet. Soil that is soggy will compact when worked and hard clumps will form when it dries. Soil that is worked when it is too dry becomes powdery. If you are in doubt about whether your soil is in good condition to work, you can use the same test you use to determine when the soil is ready to work, squeezing the soil into a ball in your hand. See idea 88 for details.

90 cultivate in autumn, too

It is a good idea to try to work your soil in fall as well as in spring. When you cultivate in fall, leave the soil surface rough in areas of the garden that are empty over the winter. Frost heaving during the winter will help bring minerals up from the subsoil and will expose insect eggs and overwintering pests to birds and killing temperatures.

91 how to avoid compaction

Never dig, cultivate, or walk on wet soil or you may cause it to compact. Dense, compacted soil provides a poor growing environment for plants; it drains poorly and roots have a difficult time penetrating and finding enough oxygen.

92 improve drainage

For better drainage in soggy soil, build raised beds and add lots of compost, leaf mold, manure, peat moss, or other organic matter to the soil in the beds. If the existing soil is of very poor quality, add some topsoil as well. In extreme cases, remove the soil to a depth of 2 feet, install drainage tiles or a layer of coarse gravel, and replace the soil.

93 better drainage for clay soil

If you have clay soil that drains poorly and puddles on the surface, work in lots of organic matter to improve its texture. Also add lime or, for faster results, agricultural gypsum to break a chemical bond that causes water to cling to soil particles.

94 shortcut pH test

Here's a quick and easy way to tell whether your soil is very alkaline. Put a couple of spoonfuls of dry soil into a jar and add an equal amount of white vinegar. Screw the lid on the jar and shake up the contents; then remove the lid and hold the jar close to your ear. If you hear a fizzing noise, your soil is quite alkaline. A faint fizzing sound means your soil is only a little alkaline. Perform a standard pH test to determine the actual level.

95 sampling soil

When preparing soil samples for a soil pH test, whether you are using a do-it-yourself test kit or sending the samples to a soil-testing service, take small samples from several different spots in the garden and mix them together. Wear gloves so that the soil samples do not come in contact with your hands; the oils in your skin could alter the test results.

96 soil pH indicators

Wild plants can be useful indicators of soil type and quality. The following weeds grow in acid soil: sorrel, dock, knotweed, wild strawberries, cinquefoil, and plantain. These weeds grow in alkaline soil: wild peppergrass, bladder campion, and goosefoot (Chenopodium species). Broom sedge, yellow toadflax, sheep sorrel, quackgrass, pineapple weed, and wild mustard indicate soil of generally poor quality.

97 adjusting soil pH

It is difficult—and foolish—to drastically change the pH of your garden soil, but you can raise or lower it a moderate degree to create more hospitable conditions for plants. To raise the pH of acid soil, work in ground limestone, wood ashes, bone meal, or crushed shells from eggs, clams, or oysters. To lower the pH of alkaline soil, add acid peat moss, cottonseed meal, oak leaf mold, pine needles, or sawdust with nitrogen. Dig the material deeply into the soil; then test again in two or three weeks.

98 the best pH for herbs

Herbs are easy to grow, and most thrive in rather poor, dry soil as long as they get lots of sun. The many kinds of thyme and sage, along with lavender and santolina, do especially well in such conditions. But for the very best herb garden, plant in soil with a pH near neutral—about 6.5 to 7.0.

99 soil for intensive gardens

Intensively planted gardens must have excellent soil in order to produce successful crops. Work lots of compost, composted manure, rock powders, and peat moss into the soil to enrich it and improve the texture. Soil that is fertile, rich in organic matter, crumbly, and moisture-retentive, but well drained, is often easiest to achieve in raised beds.

100 let earthworms work for you

Earthworms are extremely helpful in the garden; they aerate the soil with their tunneling, help break down organic matter, and leave behind their nutrient-rich castings. They can travel down as far as 6 feet, but they cannot withstand frost. If you want worms to go deep into your garden to aerate the subsoil, lay down only a thin layer of winter mulch, or do not mulch at all. The worms will have to move deeper into the soil to escape the frost line.

101 a successful rock garden

The most critical factor in the successful cultivation of rock garden plants is excellent drainage; these plants cannot tolerate soggy soil. Sandy, pebbly soils are generally best.

102 soil for a rock garden

A good soil mix for a rock garden is one part good loamy soil, one part compost, and two parts pebbles and fine gravel. Or use a mix of three parts loam and one part sharp sand; mix that in turn with two parts compost or leaf mold, two parts gravel, and one-half part crushed limestone.

103 soil for vines

Because a vine must support a lot of leaves from a relatively small patch of soil, the soil needs to be especially good. Remove stones and other debris from an area 3 feet across and 1½ to 2 feet deep surrounding the intended planting spot. Work lots of compost, leaf mold, or composted manure into the planting area; a 1- to 2-inch layer should be sufficient. If the soil is heavy clay, work in some sand as well.

104 soil in the shade

The soil in shady places tends to have an acid pH. One way to grow plants successfully in shade is to match plants to conditions; grow acid lovers like mountain laurel, azaleas, rhododendrons, camellias, shadblow, and holly in your shady areas.

105 soil for a cold frame

The soil in a cold frame should be rich and well drained. One good soil mix is one part topsoil, two parts compost or leaf mold, one part composted manure, and one part peat moss or vermiculite.

106 organic fertilizers

Organic nitrogen sources include animal manures (do *not* use pet droppings), fish meal and emulsion, cottonseed meal, and dried blood or blood meal. For potassium use wood ashes, greensand, or granite dust. Sources of phosphorus include bonemeal, rock phosphate and colloidal phosphate. Seaweed and algae products supply necessary trace elements.

107 all-purpose organic fertilizer

Here's a formula for an all-purpose organic fertilizer you can blend yourself: one part dried blood or dehydrated manure, one part bonemeal or colloidal or rock phosphate, three parts granite dust, and five parts seaweed meal.

108 organic fertilizer for flowers

Here's a formula for an organic high-phosphorus fertilizer to use in flower beds: one part dried blood or fish meal, two parts colloidal or rock phosphate, two parts bonemeal, one part seaweed meal, and three parts greensand or granite dust.

109 liquid organic fertilizer

Here's a recipe for an organic liquid fertilizer to use on vegetables growing in containers, especially leafy crops: to 1 gallon of water add a tablespoon each of liquid seaweed, fish emulsion, and dried blood or blood meal. Shake well. Use the solution to water plants every three to four weeks.

110 what to put in compost

Here are some ingredients to include in a compost pile: leaves, grass clippings, young weeds, plant prunings, vegetable peelings, eggshells, coffee grounds and used tea leaves, soil, manure (from cows, horses, sheep, pigs, or chickens), rock powders (rock phosphate and granite dust), bonemeal, seaweed, fish scraps, and hay.

111 what not to put in compost

When building a compost pile, do not include the following: oils, fats or meat products; pet manures, which may contain pathogens that will not be destroyed even in a hot pile; diseased or pest-infested plants, which will only spread the problem through the garden with the compost; weeds that have bloomed and gone to seed, (the compost will simply distribute the weed seeds throughout the garden); poisonous plants such as poison ivy, castor bean, datura, and oleander.

112 no space for compost?

If you don't have room for a compost pile, here's another way to recycle your kitchen scraps for the benefit of the garden. Once a day, put carrot tops, vegetable peelings, coffee grounds, and other compostable kitchen scraps (see Tip 110) in a blender with enough water to cover, and puree them. Dig a hole or trench in the garden, pour in the puree, and cover with dirt.

113 fast compost

Compost will be ready to use in as little as two weeks if you turn it every day, or in about a month if you turn it once a week. To make fast compost, put down a 2- to 4-inch layer of dry plant matter (shredded leaves, straw, hay, etc.), then 2 inches of "green material" (fresh manure, coffee grounds, vegetable peelings, hedge clippings), then a dusting of bonemeal and rock powder. Repeat the layers until the pile is 3 or 4 feet high. Moisten after each sequence of layers. Make the upper layers not quite as wide as the lower layers, so the pile tapers toward the top. Cover with black plastic. After a week, turn and mix the pile, moving material that had been on the outside to the inside. Fork off all the material and rebuild the pile in the same shape it was before. If the material has dried out, moisten it. Recover the pile. Turn the contents once a week until the compost is dark brown and crumbly. For even faster compost, turn the pile every day or every other day.

114 lazy gardener's compost

For a truly easy way to make compost, fill a wire bin with plant debris (pulled weeds that haven't yet gone to seed, leaves, grass clippings), dust with bonemeal, and moisten. Wet down the pile when it gets dry, but otherwise leave it alone. In a year or so, you will have finished compost.

115 for speedier compost

Shredding leaves, twigs, and other bulky compost ingredients enables them to decompose faster. You can shred leaves by running over them a few times with a power lawn mower. For twigs, branches, and other woody material, rent a shredder/clipper.

116 compost for maintenance

In an established garden with good soil, add a layer of compost ½ to 1 inch thick to the entire garden every year to maintain the soil quality. Till the compost into the soil with a rotary tiller, or by turning it under with a shovel or spade.

117 leaf compost

For a simple compost, use equal parts of fresh grass clippings and dry leaves, preferably shredded. Turn the pile with a shovel every couple of weeks, using a sharp spade or mattock to cut off and restack slices if necessary. Mix up the pile and moisten if necessary.

118 compost in a bag

City dwellers with no place for a compost bin or pile can make compost in a bag. Fill a heavy-duty plastic trash bag with alternating layers of grass clippings or kitchen wastes and leaves, sprinkling each layer with some fertilizer and lime. Moisten with water (about 4 cups), and close the bag tightly. Leave the bag outdoors during warm weather. In fall, put the bag in the basement, and the compost will be ready to use by the following spring.

119 when to add organic matter

It is important to work compost and other organic matter into the soil several months before planting, so the soil microorganisms can break down the material and make the nutrients available to plants. This head start is especially important in the case of fresh manure, because manure gets quite hot as it decomposes and can burn plant roots.

120 ashes, ashes

If you have a fireplace or wood stove, save the ashes to use in the garden. Wood ashes are a good source of potassium, and unlike some organic materials (such as rock powders), they release their nutrients quickly. Apply ashes to the soil only a day or so before planting. Spread the ashes over the soil and work them in well; their fast release of nutrients could burn delicate young plants and seeds if they make direct contact.

121 use sharp sand in soil

Sand is useful in potting mixes, for lightening the texture of soil and improving drainage. Use sharp builder's sand, not beach or river sand. Beach and river sands contain very fine particles that tend to compact rather than aerate the potting mix. Ocean beach sand also contains salts that can harm plants, especially delicate young seedlings.

122 microwave potting soil

Use your microwave oven to sterilize soil for potting mixes. For best results, the soil should be moist and crumbly—neither soggy nor dry. Put 2 pounds of soil in a plastic turkey-roasting bag. Do not seal the bag shut; it could explode. Place the bag in the oven and then microwave on high for 2½ to 3 minutes. Let the soil cool to room temperature before using it.

123 peat moss for potting

Peat moss must be moistened before it is used in potting mixes. When dry, peat moss actually repels water. The best way to dampen peat moss is to put it in a bucket, pour on some water, and work it through the moss with your hands, as if you were kneading bread dough.

124 wetting down lots of peat

To moisten an entire bag or bale of peat moss, poke several holes in the bottom of the bag and open the top. Pour water *slowly* into the top of the bag until it seeps out the holes in the bottom. Then let it stand for about twenty minutes. Press and knead the bag to help work the water into the peat. Then scoop out a handful and squeeze it; if you can squeeze any water out of the peat, it is ready to use. If it still feels dry, repeat the watering process.

125 an essential trace element

Plants need boron only in minute quantities, but if it is not present in their soil at all they will be stunted and deformed. Symptoms of boron deficiency include new shoots curling and darkening and young leaves turning deep purple or black and developing thick, brittle midribs. To add boron to deficient soil, sprinkle a little household borax over the top and scratch it in lightly.

126 save that sod

When carving a new garden out of a lawn, don't throw away the sod. Instead, pile the pieces of turf in an out-of-the-way place, stacking them in layers with like sides together—grass to grass and root to root. In a year or so, the sod will decompose into a crumbly, loamy compost that you can add to the garden or use in potting mixes.

127 when to let weeds grow

One way to get rid of a lot of weeds in a new garden is to allow them to grow before you plant it. Prepare the soil a month or so before you want to plant; then water the soil to encourage any weed seeds to sprout. When the garden is full of young weeds, use a standard hoe or a scuffle hoe to remove them. Then plant.

128 edibles for sandy soil

The best crops to grow in sandy soil are root vegetables (the light-textured soil is easy for them to penetrate); light feeders such as lettuce, spinach, and other leafy greens; members of the cabbage family; and herbs.

129 there's a fungus among us

If your garden is troubled by fungus and other soilborne

diseases, use solar sterilization to destroy the disease-causing organisms. In spring, when the sun has strengthened, soak the garden bed with water; then cover it with a heavy sheet of clear plastic (do not use black plastic—sunlight must strike the soil for the process to work). Leave the plastic in place for four to six weeks. If you have had a reasonable amount of sunny weather, the soil should be hot enough to kill just about all the pathogens in the top 1 to 1½ feet. This process will encourage weeds to grow, however, so plan on weeding before planting.

130 give tired soil a rest

If you live in a warm climate, give your soil a couple of weeks of rest after harvesting summer crops before you start planting for fall. When you garden year-round, soil can become exhausted. Work in additional organic matter after harvest to allow it time to start breaking down in the soil before you replant.

131 try a cover crop

Cover crops—or green manures, as they are sometimes called—add nitrogen to the soil, help make nutrients available to plants, improve the texture of the soil, prevent compaction, and encourage earthworms and beneficial microorganisms to colonize the soil. Rye grass, buckwheat, alfalfa, and clover are some good cover crops. Plant after the last harvest of the season or in early spring, and till the cover crop into the soil a month or so before planting the garden.

3

PLANTING

132 plant for the future

One of the most important investments any gardener can make for the future is to plant a tree. Although you may move before a young tree reaches maturity, each tree planted replaces one of the many that are lost every minute. Deforestation is harmful to the earth's ozone layer and jeopardizes our future survival. So when planning your garden, add a few trees, too.

133 pollination needs for fruit

If you plan to grow fruit, be sure to look into its pollination needs. Many fruits require cross-pollination, and in order to produce a crop, you must plant another variety to serve as a pollinator for your fruit. Good nursery catalogs and books on growing fruit provide this information.

134 herbs and flowers go together

Herbs are delightful interspersed in a flower bed or border. For easier maintenance, plant perennial herbs with perennial flowers and annuals with annuals. Flowering herbs like lavender, beebalm, and dill provide material for bouquets and arrangements; aromatic herbs such as basil, savory, anise, and tansy can be used in companion planting to repel certain insects.

135 safe planting times

There is a more reliable way to determine safe planting times in your garden than using a zone map or average-late-frost-date chart. Key your plantings to the stages of development of certain plants in the landscape (a practice known as phenology). One of the best phenological indicator plants is the lilac. Plant cool-weather crops (peas, lettuce, onions) when the lilacs have their first leaves. When they are in full bloom, it is safe to plant tender crops like tomatoes and corn.

136 more phenology

Here is another good indicator of safe planting conditions for cold-sensitive plants. It has been in use for hundreds of years; native Americans passed it along to European colonists in the New World. Plant tender crops and ornamentals when the oak leaves are as big as a squirrel's ear, in other words, when the leaves are an inch or so long. Oak trees are the last to leaf out in spring, and when they do, the danger of frost is past.

137 your own indicator plants

To devise your own set of phenological indicators, observe what is in bloom outdoors when you start seeds indoors or plant seeds or plants in the garden. Bulbs and perennials in your garden that perform reliably year after year may be good indicators of safe planting times for garden crops. For example, when daffodils bloom, start seeds indoors for tomatoes, lettuce, and other slow-growing summer crops or fast-growing spring crops.

138 heating up soil

If the weather has been unusually cold and wet in early spring and you are unable to prepare the soil for planting early crops, you may want to resort to artificial methods to warm it. Cover the planting area with a sheet of clear plastic for a week. When you have some sunny weather, the soil should be warmer and drier and, with luck, ready for planting.

139 planting by the moon

Some gardeners like to plant vegetables in accord with the phases of the moon. The theory behind moon planting is that the moon governs the movement of fluids within plants just as it does the ocean tides. If you want to try it, here's how.

Between the new moon and the first quarter, sow or transplant leafy plants and those that bear their seeds on the outside of the fruit, such as strawberries. Between the first quarter and the full moon, plant crops whose seeds develop inside the fruit: tomatoes, squash, peas, and beans. From the full moon to the last quarter, plant root vegetables. From the last quarter to the new moon, do not plant; instead, concentrate on other gardening chores.

140 why plant in fall?

Take advantage of fall planting, when you aren't as busy as you are in spring and weather conditions are usually better. You probably already plant bulbs in fall. But it is also a good time to plant shrubs, trees, hardy annuals, and a surprising number of perennials, especially late spring and summer bloomers.

141 don't start tomatoes too early

Don't be in a hurry to start tomatoes from seeds indoors. Smaller plants with six or seven leaves recover more quickly after transplanting and produce higher yields than larger seedlings. Wait until six weeks before you expect the last spring frost to sow tomato seeds, and your seedlings will be an optimal size when the time comes to put them in the garden.

142 safe planting for fall vegetables

Here's how to figure out the last date for planting fall crops. Look up the number of days to maturity (from seed packets, catalogs, or gardening books). To this number, add fourteen days to allow for plants' slower growth rate during the shorter days of late summer and early fall. Then add the number of days to transplanting for vegetables you will start indoors or in a nursery bed: for endive, lettuce and other greens, add fourteen days; for tomatoes and members of the cabbage family, add twenty-one days. For crops, such as beans, that must be picked before the first frost, add fourteen more days. Add up the total for each crop. For each crop, count backward this number of days from the average date of your first fall frost. The outcome will be the last planting date.

143 quick viability test for seeds

To make a shortcut viability test of large seeds, drop the seeds in a container of water. Good seeds will sink to the bottom; nonviable seeds will float.

144 seeds like hot water

To speed germination of many seeds, water them the first time, right after planting, with a fine spray of hot water. Thereafter, water with lukewarm or room-temperature water. Never water with cold water; germination will be slower, and growing plants can experience shock that actually slows their growth.

145 best container for seed

You can start seedlings indoors in just about anything that will hold the potting medium and provide drainage. But in tests performed a number of years ago by *Organic Gardening* magazine, a standard wooden nursery flat worked best of all.

146 better germination in summer

To promote good germination of seeds sown directly in the garden in summer:

1. Sow in moist soil, after rain or a thorough watering.
2. Plant slightly deeper than the recommended depth, and leave the surface of the planted row or block slightly lower than the surrounding soil, to collect additional moisture for the seeds and to eliminate runoff.
3. Cover with a shallow layer of straw or dry grass clippings to keep the soil from forming a crust.
4. Water as needed to keep the planting area evenly moist until germination occurs.

147 give seeds a bath

To get seeds of morning glory, moonflower, sweet peas, lupine, okra, or asparagus to germinate faster, rub the seeds between two blocks of wood covered with sandpaper. Then rub them between your hands in warm soapy water (do not use detergent). Let soak overnight, rinse, drain on paper towels, and plant.

148 give tiny seeds a good start

To improve the germination rate of tiny seeds, press them lightly into the soil but do not cover them. Sprinkle finely sieved compost, sand, or milled sphagnum moss (not peat) on top of them. Water by misting to avoid dislodging the seeds.

149 simple sowing

Most seeds will germinate if you simply place them on top of the moist starting medium and very lightly press them down or sprinkle them with a fine layer of the medium. Mist or water with a fine spray to settle them in.

150 sow fine seeds with sand

Very fine seeds, like those of begonias and lettuce, are difficult to sow evenly. To make it easier, mix the seeds with an equal volume of sand. Take a handful of the seed/sand mixture and let it sift slowly between your thumb and forefinger as you pass your hand over the soil surface; or shake the mixture of seeds and sand through a sieve or strainer; or place the seeds in a folded piece of paper and tap them out slowly with your finger.

151 presprouting pokey seeds

Soak or presprout seeds that are slow to germinate to help them sprout faster. Soak the seeds in lukewarm water overnight; then place them on a damp paper towel. Roll up the towel, wrap it in plastic wrap, and put a rubber band around each end to hold it all together. (Place the wrapped towel in a plastic bag) with a few air holes punched in it, and seal. Keep the bag out of direct light until the seeds sprout (check every few days to see if germination has occurred). Then plant the seeds in the garden, not quite as deep as the planting depth suggested on the seed packet. Handle the sprouted seeds with care; the tiny roots are extremely delicate.

152 plant shallow rather than deep

Never plant seeds too deep; they will not sprout. If you are in doubt about how deep to plant a seed, just cover it lightly. Most seeds do not need complete darkness to germinate, so it is better to plant too shallow than too deep.

153 hill planting

Planting cucumbers, squash, and melons in hills allows the soil to warm up in spring faster than it would in a flat garden. Make individual hills or a few large ones, 2 to 3 feet across and 6 to 8 inches high.

154 head off damping-off

The only way to treat damping-off, the notorious killer of seedlings, is to prevent it in the first place. Here are five preventive measures you can take:

1. Sprinkle a layer of milled sphagnum moss on top of the growing medium or soil.
2. Pasteurize sand or garden soil used in indoor seed-starting mixtures, and then be careful not to contaminate the mix when you work around the plants.
3. Make sure your hands, tools, containers, and work area are clean. Scrub previously used containers with soapy water and rinse. Soak unglazed clay pots in a solution of one part liquid chlorine bleach to nine parts water.
4. Surface-sterilize seeds by soaking them in the same strength bleach solution for one to two minutes; then drain on paper towels and plant at once.
5. Make sure seedlings have adequate growing space and good air circulation.

155 moisture for seeds

Seeds need to have soil that is constantly, evenly moist until they sprout. For seeds that take a long time to sprout, such as parsley, it can be difficult to maintain moisture. To make it easier, cover the area where these seeds are planted with a piece of moist burlap. When the burlap dries out, spray or mist it with water. You may have to do this twice a day, but it allows you to keep the soil surface moist without washing any of it away and exposing the seeds.

156 a humidity chamber for seeds

When starting seeds indoors in a flat or other container, cover the container with a sheet of plastic after planting to help keep humidity levels high. Keep the plastic from touching the soil surface (and, later, the plant foliage) by stretching it over squared-off wire hoops made of bent coat hangers, or over small wooden dowels placed in the corners of the flat. The square shape of the plastic tent allows water condensing on the inside of the plastic to drip back onto the plants instead of running down the sides of the plastic. With this tent, you may not have to water for as long as two weeks. Open the plastic for an hour or so each day to let in fresh air.

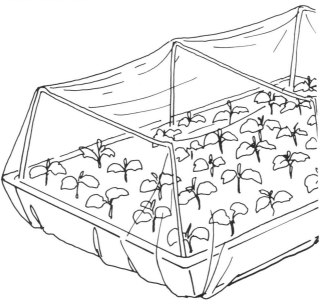

157 gentle watering

The best way to water newly planted seeds without disturbing them is to water them from the bottom. Set the flat or container in a pan of water until the soil surface feels damp.

158 seed-starting media

Here are two good recipes for seed-starting mixes: equal parts of peat moss, perlite, and vermiculite, and equal parts of peat moss and sharp sand.

159 moisten that medium

Any seed-starting medium must be moistened before seeds are planted, and in the case of a peat-based medium, this can be difficult to accomplish. Kneading water through the medium is effective, but if done too zealously, it can compact the medium and force out air. A safer—but slower—method is to put the peat in a container with drainage holes in the bottom and set the container in a pan of warm water until the top of the peat feels moist.

160 a natural fungicide

Sphagnum moss is known to have fungicidal properties. Take advantage of them to protect seedlings you start indoors (or out) from damping-off. Cover tiny seeds with a thin layer of finely milled sphagnum. For larger seeds, sprinkle the layer of sphagnum on top of the soil covering the seeds. Sphagnum can cause skin irritation if it gets into cuts, so wear gloves when working with it.

161 peat pot pointers

Peat pots are convenient and easy to use, and because you can leave seedlings in the pots when you transplant them into the garden, they minimize root disturbance and shock. Peat pots will break down in moist soil. But for the best results, tear the sides of the pot to make it easy for roots to grow through them, and be sure the pot is completely buried in the garden. If the top rim of the peat pot is above-ground, it can dry out and act as a wick, drawing moisture from the walls of the pot and the soil inside—an unhealthy situation for seedlings trying to establish themselves in the garden. On a sunny, windy day this wicking action can dry out the soil enough to water-stress the plants.

162 to block or not?

Soil blocks are great for starting seedlings indoors, especially if you will be planting lots of seeds. The blocks provide a good growing medium for roots and are inexpensive to make, after you purchase the special tool needed to make them (a small metal box equipped with a plunger to compress the soil). Soil blocks are not very high, however, so it is not a good idea to use them to start seeds of beets, carrots, turnips, or other plants that develop a long taproot.

163 catch reflected light

Seedlings need the maximum possible amount of light when growing indoors. If you are growing seedlings on windowsills, reflective surfaces near the plants will bounce additional light back onto them. White-painted walls and sills are more reflective than dark colors; a light-colored sidewalk right outside the window reflects more light than a macadam driveway. You can also line the windowsill with aluminum foil or place a foil-covered panel or a mirror between the plants and the room.

164 light but not heat for seedlings

In order to remain compact, sturdy, and vigorous, seedlings need lots of bright light but not a lot of heat. If you are starting seedlings on windowsills, use an unobstructed south window if you live in the North. If you live in the South, a south-facing windowsill may get too hot in the afternoon; grow your seedlings in an east window instead. Placing a sheer curtain between the windowpane and plants will also reduce heat. But don't put containers on *any* windowsill until the plants are up.

165 help plants out of peat pellets

If you start seeds in peat pellets, which when moistened expand into small individual peat pots encased in plastic netting, use a small scissors and cut open the plastic netting when transplanting the seedlings into the garden. Roots can then easily grow out into the surrounding soil.

166 gauging the needs of seedlings

To judge what temperatures seedlings need in order to do well indoors, think about the kinds of conditions the plants need when they mature. Plants that like cool weather, such as broccoli, cabbage, onions, and pansies, need cool conditions as seedlings: 50 to 65 degrees Fahrenheit. Tender summer plants, like eggplant, tomatoes, and impatiens, grow better with more warmth: 60 to 70 degrees Fahrenheit.

167 an efficient light garden

When you are starting seeds indoors under lights, keep the lights operating at maximum efficiency. One effective way to do this is simply to keep the lights clean—a practice that's easy to forget. Dust the fixtures and bulbs every week or two, and wipe them with a damp cloth whenever you have to replace a bulb. Replace fluorescent bulbs when they develop dark rings at the ends, before they burn out.

168 a boost for seedlings

When seedlings break through the surface of a germination medium that contains no soil or fertilizers, mist them once a week with a solution of seaweed concentrate, fish emulsion, or other liquid fertilizer diluted to one-quarter or one-half the recommended strength. If you start with quarter strength, increase the dosage to half strength after two weeks.

169 plants need their space

Whether you start seeds indoors or directly in the garden, it is important that seedlings not be crowded if they are to develop properly. It is also essential for seedlings to receive good air circulation to prevent the development of damping-off and other fungal diseases. When the leaves of adjoining seedlings begin to touch one another, it's time to transplant.

170 foiling cutworms

To protect seedlings of broccoli, cabbage, and other crops threatened by cutworms, place a cardboard collar around the base of the stem of each plant when you set the plants in the garden, or when direct-seeded plants are 1 or 2 inches tall. The collars should reach 2 or 3 inches into the soil and extend a couple of inches above the surface. Make the collars from strips of cardboard stapled together, small paper cups with the bottoms punched out, or sections of cardboard milk cartons with the tops and bottoms cut off.

171 painless thinning

An easy way to thin crowded seedlings is to use manicure scissors to snip off the stems of unwanted seedlings at ground level. That way you avoid damaging the roots of plants you want to keep when you pull up their neighbors.

172 handle with care

When transplanting small seedlings, handle them gently and always pick them up by the leaves instead of by their stems. A small plant can always grow new leaves, but if the delicate stem is damaged, the seedling may die. When transplanting, after loosening the plant in its container grasp the topmost leaves gently between your thumb and forefinger and lift the seedling carefully. Provide support under the roots with a spoon or your other hand.

173 hard to transplant seedlings

To give an early indoor start to seeds of plants that do not transplant well, one solution is to start seeds in individual peat pots and later plant the seedlings, pot and all, in the garden. Another method is to plant two or four seeds in a 4- or 5-inch pot; when the plants are ready to go into the garden, unpot them as carefully as you can and replant them as a unit, without separating them. Handle the rootball gently, and keep as much of the potting mix intact around the roots as you can. If necessary, you can thin later on to leave just the strongest plants.

174 block to prevent shock

To minimize transplant shock to seedlings growing in undivided nursery flats, block the plants a week or so before you transplant them to the garden, to separate their root systems. Use a sharp knife to cut the soil into blocks—as if you were cutting a sheet cake—with a plant in the center of each block. The cut roots will heal in a week to ten days.

55

175 separating seedlings

If you must transplant seedlings whose roots have grown into each other in an overcrowded flat, do not try to disentangle the roots by pulling them apart; that would damage the delicate roots and set back the plants' growth. Instead, remove the plants from the flat in a group, and cut them apart with a sharp knife, disturbing the roots as little as possible. Better yet, block the seedlings in the flats before transplanting, as described in idea 176.

176 when to transplant

A cloudy day is best for transplanting seedlings outdoors. If it is summertime and the weather is hot, even if the sun is not out, do the transplanting in the morning or late in the day. Water after planting to settle the soil around the roots. Late in the afternoon of the day before you expect to transplant, water the planting area and the seedlings.

177 hardening off

Seedlings started indoors should be gradually acclimated to outdoor conditions before you plant them in the garden, a process known as hardening off. Hardening off lessens transplant shock and allows the young plants to recover quickly and resume growing in the garden. Even in summer, seedlings need time to adjust to the brighter, hotter conditions outdoors.

To harden off seedlings, move them outdoors in their containers, placing them in a lightly shaded location. Leave the plants outdoors for only a few hours the first day; then bring them back inside. Over a week to ten days, leave the plants outside a little longer each day, until the last night, when you can leave them outdoors overnight. The seedlings will then be ready for transplanting, if weather conditions permit.

Don't forget to water the plants when they need it during the hardening-off period.

178 how deep to transplant

When transplanting a seedling with an upright, branched stem that has the growing point at the top of the stem (such as a tomato or an eggplant), transplant the seedling deeper than it was previously growing—almost up to the lowest leaves—and additional roots will form on the newly buried part of the stem. Transplant seedlings that grow in a rosette form with the leaves gathered around a central growing point (like lettuce) at the same depth they were growing previously. If you plant deeper and inadvertently bury the growing point, the plant will die.

179 letting transplants settle in

Cut back on fertilizing and watering for the first several days after transplanting, to give the plants time to become established in their new locations. They need a few days' rest before they can resume growing. Providing shade is also helpful during this transition period.

180 relief for potbound plants

When transplanting plants that have become severely potbound, use a sharp knife to make several vertical cuts up through the rootball and gently spread some of the roots apart before putting the plant in the garden or in a larger pot. If you notice any roots wrapped around other roots or around the stem, cut them off.

181 the right way to unpot

To remove a stubborn plant from its pot, do *not* pull on the stem. Turn the pot upside down, supporting the soil around the stem with one hand, and tap the bottom of the pot with the handle of a trowel or other tool. If the rootball still does not slide easily out of the pot, set the pot upright and run the blade of a dull knife around the inside of the pot. Then invert the pot and slide out the plant.

182 handling container plants

There's an easy way to make sure the roots of container-grown plants travel down and out into the surrounding soil when planting them in the garden. Unpot the plant and lay it on your open palm, with the top growth pointing toward your elbow. With your other hand, very gently tease apart some of the larger roots. Then place the plant carefully in the hole.

183 getting rid of air pockets

It is important to eliminate air pockets in the soil around newly planted trees and shrubs so the roots make good contact with the soil. When planting, fill the hole partway with soil and work the soil around the roots with your fingers. When the hole is half full, rock the plant back and forth to help settle it. When the hole is two-thirds full, water to settle the soil and get rid of air pockets; then fill the hole the rest of the way.

184 a quicker transition

To help a container-grown plant get established in a garden where the soil is heavy and dense, make a vertical cut up into the bottom center of the rootball, and spread the two halves of the rootball apart when planting. The cut exposes more roots to the soil, and new feeder roots will form faster.

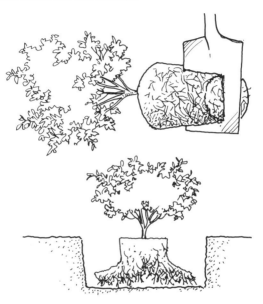

185 midseason transplanting

When setting out transplants in midseason, dig the hole a little deeper than necessary and put a trowelful of compost, leaf mold, used tea leaves, or even shredded newspaper (black-and-white pages only) in the bottom of the hole. Fill the hole to the top with water, and let the water drain off. Then set the plant in the hole and fill the hole almost to the top with water, and let the water drain off. Then fill the hole almost to the top with soil. Firm the soil around the roots and leave a slight depression around the stem to hold water.

186 transplanting mature plants

It's easy to dig and pot herbs or other plants from your outdoor garden to bring them indoors for winter. Two weeks before you expect to dig them, push a spade as far as it will go into the soil all around the plant. Place the spade about halfway between the main stem and the outer edge of the plant's top growth. Like blocking seedlings, this procedure severs the roots and prepares them for transplanting. Keep the soil moist until you dig the plants.

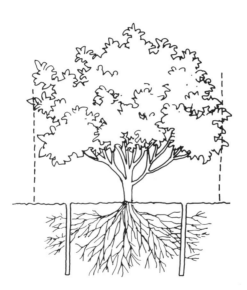

187 the size of the hole

Here's a rule of thumb for determining how large a hole to dig for a tree or shrub. If the plant is bare-rooted, make the hole 1½ times as deep and wide as the roots would extend if they were stretched out straight. If the plant is balled-and-burlapped or container-grown, make the hole 6 inches bigger than the root-ball in all directions. It is always better to dig the hole too large than too small.

188 balled-and-burlapped trees

When you plant a balled-and-burlapped tree with the rootball wrapped in real burlap, make several cuts in the burlap to allow the roots to grow through until the burlap decomposes. Roll back the top of the burlap so none of it will extend above the soil surface when the planting hole is filled. In addition, loosen or unwrap the twine or rope from around the rootball before filling the hole. If the rootball is wrapped in a burlap substitute, remove the wrapping entirely before planting.

189 remove that tag

When you plant a tree or shrub, be sure to remove the metal nursery tag from the stem or branch. When left on the plant, the tag will eventually constrict the growth of the branch or cut into the bark and injure the plant, an invitation for pests and diseases to attack. If you are afraid of forgetting the name of the variety, make a note in your garden journal, or make a plant label to put in the ground.

190 help for a young tree

Newly planted trees are usually held in place with stakes and guy wires until the roots establish a good hold in the soil. But the support prevents the tree from bending with the wind, which it needs to do in order to grow strong. On the other hand, if the tree were to be unstaked, it would be very vulnerable to wind damage. The solution is to remove the supporting devices as early as is feasible. If you planted in spring, remove the wires in late summer or fall.

191 handling bare-root stock

Many trees and shrubs are sold in bare-root form, and it is important to keep the roots from drying out both before and after planting. If you cannot plant when you receive the shrubs or trees, set them in a shallow trench on an angle, and cover the roots with soil. Then soak the roots overnight in a bucket of muddy water before planting. To seal in moisture and protect the roots after planting, dip them in a bucket containing a slurry of water, manure, and clayey soil before setting the plant in the hole.

192 planting through plastic

If you are using black plastic mulch, it must be installed before you plant. To set in plants, make an X-shaped slit rather than a hole through which to plant, so you can draw the plastic back around the stem, leaving no uncovered ground where weeds could grow.

193 pick the best plants

Here are some tips for picking plants at the garden center:

- Avoid large plants in small containers; they will be rootbound, and growth will be slowed.
- Avoid plants already in bloom; they will suffer more transplant shock and adapt slowly to the garden.
- Don't buy lanky, spindly plants with small leaves spaced too widely on the stems; they haven't had enough light.
- Don't buy yellowish, pale, or poorly colored plants; they are undernourished
- Don't buy limp, flaccid plants; they're too dry.
- Don't buy plants with pest or disease symptoms; examine plants carefully before you buy, especially leaf axils, the undersides of leaves, and the growing tip. Check for damaged, distorted, and misshapen leaves.
- Do buy seedlings that are stocky, sturdy, and compact, with a firm texture, bushy growth, and a good green color. These plants are healthy and will make the transition easily.

194 pick the best bulbs

If you buy bulbs at the garden center, examine them carefully before you buy; if you order by mail, look them over before planting. Here's what to look for:

- The bulbs should feel solid and heavy; if they feel very light they are probably dried out.
- They should be firm all over with no soft, shriveled spots (exceptions are anemones and winter aconites, which have wrinkly roots that are soaked in water before planting).
- They should have no moldy, discolored, or dark spots.
- On bulbs having a basal plate, the base should be firm.
- There should be no holes or other signs of insect damage.

- Try not to buy bulbs that have already sprouted; it is better if they grow roots first.

195 keeping mint under control

Mints are delightful in an herb garden, but most of them are very invasive and can spread all over the garden unless you keep them in check. A painless way to control their rampant growth is to plant them in bottomless wood boxes 1 foot square by 1 foot deep to contain the invasive rhizomes. Or plant them in a wide container buried up to its rim in the soil.

196 a vine-covered cottage

If you want to grow vines on a wood-shingled or wood-sided house, put up a trellis in front of the wall and train the vines on that. Vines growing directly on the wood will eventually cause moisture damage.

197 saving vines from leaf burn

Evergreen vines growing on walls in northern gardens often suffer leaf burn in late winter. Water lost from the leaves cannot be replaced by the roots because the ground is frozen. Planting evergreen vines on the north or east side of the house minimizes leaf burn. Burning will be worse on vines growing on the south side, where additional sun exposure dries out the leaves more severely.

198 plant for your pets

If you have cats, plant a patch of catnip for them, to keep them out of the main garden. Cats also like the young leaves of oats. Dogs like oats, too, but as a special treat for your dog, plant a small patch of fescue grass.

199 root cuttings

Root cuttings are a good way to propagate woody vines, trees, shrubs, and herbaceous perennials. They work especially well for plants that produce suckers from the roots (oriental poppies, garden phlox, plumbago, wisteria, trumpet creeper, raspberries, and blackberries, for example). But do not take root cuttings from plants that have been grafted, or you will end up with the rootstock parent plant rather than the top-growth plant.

200 taking softwood cuttings

Softwood cuttings, from perennials, shrubs, or greenhouse plants, should be planted right away, but when you take them is also critical; if they are even a few weeks too old they won't root. If you cannot plant the cuttings immediately, wrap the bottoms of the cuttings in moist paper towels and then in plastic wrap. You can hold them like this for several hours or even an entire day.

201 when to take softwood cuttings

Softwood cuttings can be used to propagate bedding plants and some perennials, shrubs, and trees. Take the cuttings from shoots in their first year of growth, when the plant is about halfway through the current growing season, and when the stems are firm but still flexible. If the stem crushes when bent, it is too young to use as a cutting; if it snaps, it is too old. Choose a healthy side shoot of medium vigor; do not use the largest, most vigorous shoots.

202 taking hardwood cuttings

You can use hardwood cuttings to propagate fruit trees, hardy deciduous shrubs and vines, evergreen groundcovers, and some ornamental trees. Take them in fall when the plant is dormant, from the ends of healthy new branches or canes that have grown from the base of the plant.

203 tips for azalea cuttings

Take cuttings of azaleas, rhododendrons, and other broad-leaved evergreens in October-November (or December-January in warm climates). Take mature shoots 3 to 5 inches long from the tips of branches (cuttings will be shorter from plants that are dwarf or compact varieties). Cut just below a node, if possible, and make all the cuttings the same length. Store the cuttings upright until planting time, so the chemicals that cause roots to form will move toward the bottom of each cutting.

204 conifer cuttings determine shapes

If you want to propagate a yew or other coniferous evergreen from cuttings, think about the form you would like the new plants to take. Cuttings from side shoots tend to produce plants with a bushy, spreading habit. Cuttings taken from upright shoots tend to develop into upright plants with a more vertical form.

205 moving cuttings from water to soil

When you root plant cuttings of coleus, ivy, begonias, geraniums, or other plants in water, allow the roots to form and then add soil or sand gradually over a few weeks, so the roots can adapt slowly to their new environment.

206 rooting media

Some good media for rooting cuttings are equal parts of sharp builder's sand and peat moss, or peat and perlite, or perlite and vermiculite. The medium you use should be evenly moist but not soggy.

207 the right position for root cuttings

Set root cuttings from fleshy, thick roots upright in the rooting medium to root, with the top of the cutting positioned just below the surface of the medium. Set cuttings taken from delicate, thin-rooted plants horizontally and about 2 inches deep in a fine-textured medium. When taking root cuttings, cut the upper end on an angle and the lower end straight across so you will remember which end is up when you plant them in the rooting medium.

208 large-leaved cuttings

If you are rooting cuttings of plants that have long or large leaves, you can cut off as much as half of each leaf to allow more cuttings to fit in the flat or other rooting area. Also be sure to remove the lower leaves entirely as well as any flower buds that may be present.

209 rooting softwood cuttings

Root softwood cuttings in a moist medium that is light-textured and sterile and that contains no soil. After removing the leaves from the bottom third of the cutting, stand it upright in the rooting medium up to one-quarter to one-half its length; never cover more than half the cutting's stem.

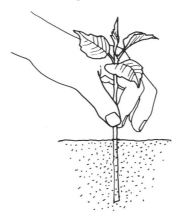

210 a special pot for cuttings

While a small number of cuttings are rooting, keep the medium evenly moist with a special pot. You will need two unglazed clay pots: a wide, shallow bulb pan 6 to 7 inches in diameter and a small pot about 2½ inches across. Plug the drainage hole in the small pot and place the pot inside the bulb pan. Fill the space between the two pots with moist rooting medium, and plant the cuttings close to the small pot. Fill the small pot with water and keep it filled until the cuttings root. Water will seep slowly through the walls of the small pot to keep the medium moist.

To check whether the cuttings have rooted, twist the small pot to keep the medium in place, then lift up the pot and look for roots.

211 a homemade propagation unit

To keep humidity high for cuttings, build a propagation unit. Construct a wooden box, with a hinged lid, that is deep enough to accommodate your containers, the cuttings, and a fluorescent light fixture under the lid. Allow about 6 inches between the fluorescent tube and the tops of the cuttings. Install two self-mounting 40-watt fluorescent fixtures on the inside of the box lid. Put the box where the temperature is at least 65 degrees Fahrenheit. Plant the cuttings, put them in the box, close the lid, and turn on the lights for twelve hours a day. Keep the rooting medium moist but not soggy.

212 shade for cuttings

When rooting cuttings outdoors in the garden or in a cold frame, cover them with shade netting or cheese-cloth during their first week to ten days outdoors to conserve soil moisture as the cuttings settle in. After that, most cuttings, except for those from broad-leaved evergreens, root best when given some sun.

213 hormone hints

If you use a rooting hormone powder to encourage hardwood or softwood cuttings to root more quickly, do *not* dip the end of the cutting into the packet of hormone powder. If the cutting carries any disease pathogens, it will contaminate the powder and any other cutting dipped into it. Instead, pour a small amount of powder into a clean container for each cutting you dip.

214 what to layer

Layering is a good propagation method for many plants and requires no special tools or complicated procedures. It will work for a variety of plants that have flexible stems. Evergreen azaleas, blackberries, raspberries, grapes, dianthus, ivy, clematis, wisteria, hydrangea, magnolia, lilac, and vinca (periwinkle) are some plants that can be layered.

215 soil tips for layering

For layering to work best, the soil around the plant to be layered must be loose and crumbly. If the soil is heavy or of poor quality, carefully remove soil to a depth of several inches around the top of the plant (try to disturb the roots as little as possible). Mix the soil with compost or leaf mold, peat moss, and sand; then fill in around the roots with the improved soil mix.

216 tip layering

Tip layering is the simplest method for producing new plants by layering. It can be used with plants that can form roots at the ends of their stems, such as forsythia, raspberry, and blackberry. Bend some of the branches down to the ground, hold their tips in place with pegs or stones, and cover the tips with soil. Roots will form in a few months. When they do, you can sever and transplant the new plant.

217 simple layering

Simple layering will produce one new plant from each shoot layered from the parent plant. Choose a low, flexible stem and bend it down to the ground. Bend the stem in the opposite direction from the way it grows, so it will not snap off at the base. Make a slit in the soil 5 to 6 inches from the tip of the stem. To make the slit, insert the tip of a spade in the soil and push back and forth on the handle a few times. Bend the stem to the ground, twisting it slightly, and place it in the slit. Hold it in place with a forked peg, a *U*-shaped pin, or a stone. Bend the tip of the shoot so it faces up and at least 3 inches of it protrude from the soil. Cover the buried portion of the stem with improved soil mix, and pack the soil well around the stem. Do not sever the new plant from the parent until roots have formed.

218 serpentine layering for vines

One of the most productive ways to propagate woody vines such as ivy, clematis, wisteria, climbing honeysuckle, and grape is by serpentine or compound layering. Choose a low-growing, flexible stem to layer. Dig a narrow, 6-inch-deep trench in which to lay the stem. Bend the stem in a series of curves, so every other node is in the trench. Cover these nodes with soil, alternating buried and exposed nodes along the length of the stem. The following spring or fall (depending on what time of year you began the process), when the new plants have rooted, sever the old stem on either side of the buried nodes, and dig up and transplant the new plants.

219 best time for layering

Perform simple, compound, or serpentine layering in early spring, while the plant is still dormant, as soon as the soil can be worked. For tip layering and mound or stool layering, use shoots from the current season's growth and start the process in late spring, when the shoots are several inches long. Do air layering in late spring or early summer.

220 shoots for layering

Use one-year-old shoots for layering. If the plant has been pruned regularly, it should have lots of healthy year-old wood. But if the plant has been left unpruned for several years, you must get it to produce new shoots before you can layer it. Prune the plant; then feed it with compost and an all-purpose fertilizer to stimulate new growth. Next year you can layer the new shoots.

221 faster rooting during layering

To encourage plants to root faster during layering, remove a 1-inch-wide strip of bark from around the stem to be layered, at the point where it will be buried under the soil. Or instead, make a diagonal cut about halfway through the stem on the underside, and place a wooden matchstick or toothpick in the cut to hold it open. Girdling or wounding the stem in this manner promotes the formation of callus tissue, which is needed for rooting to occur. Dusting the injured part of the stem with rooting hormone powder will speed root formation even more.

222 homemade grafting wax

Here's a recipe for grafting wax that can be used on fruiting or ornamental trees. You will need one part tallow, two parts beeswax, and four parts broken resin. Melt the tallow in a heavy pot; then add the beeswax and melt it. When the beeswax is melted, add the resin. Keep at a slow boil for a half hour, and stir occasionally. Pour the wax into a container of cold water when it has cooled. Knead it and pull it until it turns the color of straw and develops a finely grained appearance. Divide the wax into several pieces and wrap each piece in waxed paper. Always grease your hands before you handle the wax. The wax will harden while stored but will soften up in your hands.

4

MAINTENANCE

223 a test for when to water

The old 1-inch-of-water-a-week rule does not work for all gardens in all locations. Plants in sandy soils need more water than plants in clay soils; and gardens in hot, dry climates need more water than gardens in cool, cloudy locations. The best way to determine when your garden needs water is to stick a finger down into the soil. When the soil feels dry 2 inches below the surface, it's time to water.

224 how much water?

On an average, it will take roughly a half gallon of water per square foot of garden space, given slowly, to thoroughly moisten dry soil. A 10×10-foot garden requires about 50 gallons.

225 deep watering

Here's an effective way to deliver water to the lower root zone of large plants. Punch several small holes in the bottoms of tin cans and sink the cans into the ground next to the plants (to avoid damaging roots, put the cans in when the plants are still small). Fill the cans with water, and it will drip out slowly and soak deep into the soil.

226 cultivate to conserve water

Regularly hoeing or cultivating prevents a crust from forming on top of soil and allows the soil to soak up water more efficiently.

227 efficient watering

Plants that are not succulents or cacti need regular moisture in order to grow at a steady pace. But it is imperative that all gardeners conserve water and not waste this most precious resource. To use water efficiently, water at ground level rather than from above, so the water goes directly to the root zone, where it is needed. Soaker hoses and drip irrigation systems both deliver water directly to roots. If you must water with a conventional hose or overhead sprinkler, do it in the morning or late afternoon so water evaporation is kept to a minimum.

228 conserving water

Here are some ways to save water in the garden:

- Make sure your garden soil contains lots of organic matter.
- Make a shallow depression in the soil around the base of each plant to catch and hold rain and runoff water.
- Plant more for spring and fall, less for summer.
- Plant drought-tolerant shrubs, flowers, herbs, and vegetables.
- Plant in blocks instead of rows to confine necessary watering to a smaller area.

229 unclogging drip systems

If you have hard water, the emitters on your drip irrigation system may become clogged with deposits of calcium carbonate. Instead of throwing out the emitters and buying new ones, soak them in vinegar. As an acid, vinegar will dissolve the deposits.

230 moisture zones

Another way to conserve water is to group your plants in different "moisture zones." Place the plants that need the most water closest to the house, where you can get to them easily. Plants that need the least water can be planted farthest from the house.

231 recycle household water

Conserve water by recycling some of your household water in the garden. Catch water dripping from air conditioners and rain gutters, run it through a filter, and use it to water plants. Empty the dehumidifier into the garden. Look into recycling graywater that has been used for showers, dishwashing, and laundry. Graywater is generally safe for plants if you use detergents that contain no boron or chlorine. But check local ordinances and building codes for collection system requirements.

232 don't water at noon

Water the garden in the morning or late in the day (but early enough so plant leaves dry before dark). Avoid watering at noon; too much water will be lost to evaporation, and water droplets clinging to leaves can act like little lenses, focusing the sun's rays and actually burning foliage. Don't water at night, either; wet foliage at night invites fungi, mold, and mildew.

233 the peril of overwatering

Too much water is as bad for plants as too little. Roots can suffocate in soggy soil for lack of oxygen and will eventually rot. When you water, water deeply and thoroughly, but let the soil dry out somewhat between waterings. It is better to give plants too little water (within reason) than too much.

234 symptoms of overwatering

The leaves of plants that are overwatered wilt, turn yellow, and eventually fall from the plant. In some cases, the tips of the leaves turn brown and brittle. If the problem is severe, the leaves will start to rot, beginning with the lowest leaves. The base of the stem may also rot.

235 clues to water needs

If you are unfamiliar with a plant's water needs, examine its leaves. As a rule, trees and shrubs whose leaves are small and either waxy or covered with hair will tolerate drought. Many silver and gray-leaved plants also like dry, sunny conditions.

236 when water is most critical

It is especially important for plants to get enough water early in the season, when they are doing most of their growing and developing. It is also important for vegetables to get adequate water when the plants are blooming and setting fruit. Later in the season, when plants are more mature, they are better able to tolerate drought.

237 tap water for plants

If you are concerned about possible ill effects of the chlorine in tap water on seedlings and delicate plants, all you need to do is let the water stand at room temperature in an open container for twenty-four hours before using it to water them. The chlorine will escape into the air and dissipate (so will fluorine). Letting the water warm to room temperature is a good idea anyway; cold water can shock plants.

238 watch out for wilting

Many plants wilt during hot summer afternoons and recover in the evening when the temperature drops. But if you see plants wilt late at night or in the morning, water them right away; their need is critical.

239 reviving wilted plants

Seedlings in small pots and plants in containers outdoors can dry out quickly. The first sign is limp, droopy leaves. If the wilting is not severe, you can usually revive the plants by watering them, misting the foliage, and moving them out of direct sun. The plants will probably suffer a slowdown of their growth because of the water stress, but they will survive.

240 low-tech drip irrigation

To supply steady moisture to a few moisture-sensitive plants, make a homemade drip irrigator from a plastic gallon milk jug. Punch a few small holes in the bottom of the jug, and partially bury the jug in the garden between sensitive plants. Fill the jug with lukewarm water. The water will drip slowly into the soil over several days. Refill the jug when it is empty. To feed plants at the same time, put a scoop of compost or manure in the jug before filling it with water, or use a solution of fish emulsion, seaweed concentrate, or other liquid fertilizer.

241 absentee watering

Here's an old-timer's trick for watering indoor seedlings and potted plants when you're away from home. You will need an old table and a heavy blanket.

Soak the blanket in warm water until it is thoroughly wet. Spread the blanket over the table, and let one end hang down to the floor. Bunch up that end and place it in a bucket of water. Set the container of plants (they must have drainage holes that are not covered by pebbles or potsherds) on top of the blanket. Capillary action will keep the blanket moist, and the plants will receive continuous bottom watering.

For a somewhat neater system, purchase capillary matting and set it up with a generous water reservoir.

242 predicting rain

When there is a ring close around the moon, rain is on the way but will not arrive for several days. When the ring around the moon is farther out, expect rain soon.

243 watch the clouds

Everyone knows that a sky full of dark clouds usually means rain. What you might not know is that the low-

er the clouds are in the sky, the sooner the rain will
come.

244 plants that predict rain

Watching certain plants in the landscape can tell you
when rain is on the way. Field daisies, dandelions, and
scarlet pimpernels close up when rain is near, and
milkweed closes at night before bad weather. Lilacs,
sugar maples, poplars, sycamores, and cottonwoods
all show the light-colored undersides of their leaves
before rain.

245 animals forecast rain

Animal behavior is another reliable indicator of stormy
weather on the way. Watch for the following:

- Cows gather together in the field and face in the
  same direction, with their tails to the wind.
- Spiders spin short webs.
- Bees stay close to the hive.
- Birds stay in the lower branches of trees, don't fly
  much, and stop singing.
- Fish stay closer than usual to the water surface and
  can be seen splashing around.

246 don't overfeed

For plants, as for people, too much food is unhealthy.
Overfertilizing plants encourages them to sprout weak
shoots that are very susceptible to damage from pests.
Where fertilizing is concerned, it is better to err on the
side of caution and allow plants to grow more slowly
rather than pushing them too fast.

247 magic potion for an earlier harvest

To get an earlier harvest from tomatoes, eggplant, or
peppers, make a solution of 2 tablespoons Epsom
salts to 1 gallon of water. When each plant begins

flowering, give it 2 cups of the solution. The extra magnesium stimulates the plants.

248 best time to fertilize

The best time to fertilize plants with a dry fertilizer is right before rain.

249 uses for wood ashes

If you have a wood stove or fireplace, save the ashes to use in the garden. They are a good source of potassium; can be scattered around carrots, radishes, and onions to keep away root maggots; and are said to improve the flavor of potatoes. They also raise soil pH, so if you apply lots of wood ashes, test the pH a few weeks later to make sure it is still acceptable.

250 winter mulches

If you wish to spread a winter mulch over the perennial garden in fall, do not be too hasty to apply it. The object of a winter mulch is to keep the soil frozen, preventing alternate freezing and thawing that can heave dormant roots and crowns out of the soil. Even under a mulch, exposed roots may die. Wait until the ground freezes to lay winter mulches.

251 removing winter mulch

Start removing winter mulches from the garden when the soil begins to thaw in early spring. If you leave the mulch in place as the weather warms, it will keep the soil colder longer and delay planting.

252 when to mulch

It is important not to lay summer mulch too early in spring. Let the soil warm up before you mulch; wait until several weeks after the last frost. If you mulch while the soil is still cold, the mulch will keep the soil cold longer; seeds will be reluctant to germinate, and plants will grow slowly.

253 how deep to mulch

The best depth for a summer mulch depends on the type of material used. If you are mulching with a fine-textured material such as buckwheat or cocoa bean hulls, sawdust, or dry grass clippings, a 2- to 3-inch layer is sufficient. Coarse material such as straw or unshredded leaves should be 8 or even 10 inches deep. Shredded leaves, bark chips, and other medium-textured mulches should be about 4 inches deep for maximum effectiveness.

254 using organic mulches

Organic mulches such as hay, straw, buckwheat hulls, and wood chips are extremely useful in the garden. They slow the evaporation of moisture from the soil and help keep the soil cooler in summer. When they decompose, they add organic matter to the garden. But these mulches also offer excellent hiding places for slugs, earwigs, and sowbugs. If your garden harbors large populations of these critters, it would be wise to eliminate the mulch to provide fewer homes for them.

255 newspaper mulch

Newspaper makes a very effective mulch; it holds moisture well, eliminates weeds, and provides a barrier to pests. To mulch with newspaper, lay down six to eight layers of black-and-white sheets. Anchor the papers with rocks, or cover them with soil to hide them. The paper will eventually decompose.

256 keeping mulch where you want it

The best way to keep mulch in place is to keep it even with the surrounding area. Make the soil level in the garden a couple of inches below an adjacent lawn or walkway to allow for the mulch. If you simply lay the mulch on top of a garden that is the same height as the lawn or walkway—as most people do—it may wash into the lawn or path during heavy rains. If you garden in raised beds, you will probably find that mulch washes into the paths between the beds and will have to be scooped up with a shovel after a rainstorm. Lining the sides of the bed with railroad ties, bricks, or stones can help keep the mulch in place.

257 wood-based mulches

If you mulch your garden with wood chips, sawdust, bark chips, or another woody material, work high-nitrogen fertilizer (such as cottonseed meal, dried blood, or manure, if you garden organically) into the top layer of soil before you lay the mulch. These woody mulches take nitrogen from the soil when they decompose and may deprive your plants unless you compensate for the loss.

258 insect-repelling mulch

If your vegetable garden is troubled by aphids and other small insects, try mulching with aluminum foil. Bugs will avoid the shiny surface. The foil bounces extra light onto plants as well.

259 too much mulch

Mulch is great, but too much of it can do more harm than good. If you pile mulch a foot deep around the base of a tree or shrub, it may encourage cankers and hinder the plant's growth. Also, mulch that is too deep may ferment in summer, causing the formation of alcohol, too much of which will poison your plants. A summer mulch is usually effective at 1 or 2 inches deep. Except when using coarse material such as straw or unshredded leaves, it should never be deeper than 4 inches.

260 slugs and mulch shouldn't mix

If you want to mulch your garden but have problems with slugs, try mulching with shredded pine bark. Slugs don't like the rough texture and will stay out of the garden.

261 balance acid mulches

Unless you are growing acid-loving plants, counteract the acidity of a pine-bark or pine-needle mulch by working into the soil a pound of lime (preferably dolomitic limestone) for each square yard of garden before you lay the mulch.

262 mulching with plastic

A black plastic mulch is a very effective way to keep weeds down. Lay the plastic over an entire garden bed. To plant, cut X-shaped slits and fold back the pieces. When the plant is in place, close the plastic around the stem. Cover the plastic with pebbles or wood chips to hide it. An underground drip irrigation system is the best way to water.

263 keeping paths weed-free

To eliminate weeds from dirt paths during a stretch of dry weather, sprinkle them heavily with kosher or regular table salt (covering the weeds until they look white), and then do not disturb them until they die. Scrape up the excess salt before rain carries it into the garden or lawn.

264 effective weeding

To get rid of weeds once and for all, do not break the plants off at ground level; they will only grow back. You must remove the roots, too. Never let weeds go to seed in the garden or you will have many more than you did before. If you use a hoe or cultivator instead of pulling weeds by hand, do it at least once a week, and avoid using it around shallow-rooted plants; it is best to pull weeds growing close to plants by hand.

265 when to prune

The best time to prune most trees and shrubs is in early spring, before the buds start to swell and the new season's growth begins.

266 pruning young trees

Young fruit trees need careful pruning to leave a good framework of "scaffold" branches to support the tree's future growth. To form the scaffold, choose branches growing at as close as possible to a 90-degree angle from the trunk, and evenly distributed radially around the trunk.

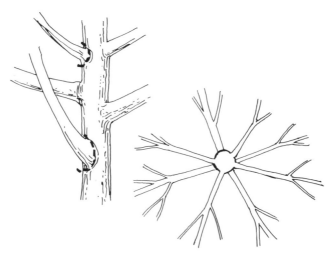

267 pruning large branches

When removing a large branch from a tree, do *not* cut it off right up to the trunk. Contrary to traditional advice, experts have found that leaving the collar (the slightly thickened ring where the branch meets the trunk) allows callus to form more quickly and decreases the chance that disease will attack the exposed trunk wood. Do not coat the open wound with wound dressing or pitch or paint; closing off the raw wood from air creates a hospitable environment for bacteria and disease pathogens around the sealed area.

268 pruning apple and pear trees

Apples and pears are often pruned so that they have a central leader, a dominant main upright shoot. To prune these trees, cut back the whip (the unbranched stem) at planting time. When shoots develop from the topmost buds, choose the strongest to be the leader. Remove the other shoots while the wood is still soft. In following years, cut off shoots that compete with the leader.

269 don't top your trees

Many people "top" trees that get too tall for their allotted space, or that block a view, by lopping off the tops of the branches. Topping is never a good idea; besides looking awful, it weakens the tree and shortens its life. Branches either die back or send up lots of weak new shoots that are likely to snap off in strong wind or, if they survive, to grow as tall as the tree was before topping. Choose trees carefully, paying close attention to their growth habits, and practice regular, correct pruning to avoid topping.

270 pruning a sick tree

When a plant is suffering from a disease that affects part, but not all of it, you can prune away the diseased parts to save the plant. Do not prune when the tree or shrub is wet; you will only spread the problem. Cut 4 to 6 inches below the diseased wood, where the plant is healthy. Dip your tools in rubbing alcohol after each cut to sterilize them.

271 first aid for a damaged tree

When a tree is injured by a collision with a car or other object, you can give it first aid. Place a bandage of black plastic over the wound (one thickness of 4-mil plastic, or several layers of thinner plastic) within two weeks after the accident. Secure the bandage with electrical tape at the top and bottom. The bandage will help the wound to grow shut and will help prevent decay.

272 prune to control growth

When you prune a tree or shrub you can control the direction of its growth. If you prune a branch just above a bud on the outer side of the branch, the new stem will grow outward. Prune this way to encourage an open-centered form. If you prune just above a bud on the inner side of the branch, the new stem will grow inward. Prune to inner buds to create a denser, bushier form.

273 the right cut controls growth

If you make a vertical incision in a trunk's cambium layer (the layer of smooth tissue between the bark and the wood) right above a branch, the branch will grow more slowly. If you make the cut right below the branch, the branch will grow more quickly. Make the incision as growth begins in spring. It should be as long as the diameter of the branch plus an inch on either side of the branch.

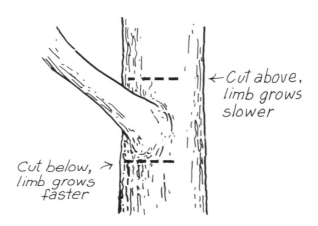

←Cut above, limb grows slower

Cut below, → limb grows faster

274 when to prune evergreens

Needled evergreen trees and shrubs can be pruned anytime except late summer. If you prune in late summer, you could stimulate new shoots to grow that will not have time to harden before frost and will be killed.

275 a natural look for evergreens

To prune conifers to an informal—but tidy—shape, step back from the shrub or tree and squint to look at its natural silhouette. Prune back the tips of branches that stick out beyond most of the other branches, and leave the others alone.

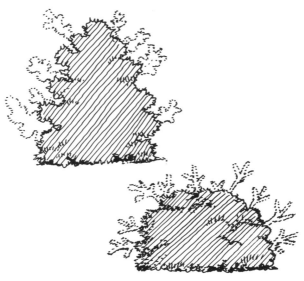

276 restoring rhododendrons

If your rhododendrons look sparse and leggy, careful pruning will make them bushier. Prune off the rosette of leaves at the end of each stem, cutting back to just above a lower group of leaves. New shoots will develop in the leaf axils.

277 don't pick bulb foliage

After spring bulbs have bloomed, their foliage is left behind. The leaves aren't terribly attractive, and it's tempting to remove them. But don't. The foliage needs to develop and mature fully in order to nourish the bulb for its next flowering. When the leaves yellow and start to dry out, it is safe to remove them. This rule does not apply to fritillaries and crown imperials; do not remove their leaves even when the leaves are dry. Planting annuals among the bulbs will help hide the foliage.

278 shaping for a hedge

Hedges are usually clipped into square shapes, with a flat top and straight vertical sides. But a much better shape is one that has a rounded or narrow top and sides that slant outward. This shape allows all the leaves to get sun, and helps keep snow from piling up on top of the hedge in winter.

279 deadhead the right way

Cut spent flower stalks of plants with leafless stems (such as daylilies) back to a couple of inches from the ground.

For plants with basal leaves (achillea and salvia, for example), cut back flower stems to right above the foliage.

Where flowers are carried amid the leaves, just pick off the dead flowers.

280 pinch mums for better bloom

Your chrysanthemums will put on their best show if you pinch them during the growing season. Pinch back the tips of the stems about ½ inch when the plants are about 6 inches tall. Repeat the pinching every two weeks until the middle of July, or August in warm climates. Pinching delays bloom slightly, but produces more flowers.

281 keep low growers happy

For healthier, bushier plants and the best bloom next year, cut back low-growing spring-flowering perennials halfway to the ground when they finish blooming. Moss pinks, evergreen candytuft, and rock cress are three plants that benefit from this treatment.

282 saving seeds

If you plan to collect and save your own seeds from open-pollinated and nonhybrid varieties of vegetables, herbs, or flowers, carefully choose the plants whose seeds you will save. Select the most productive, vigorous plants at the peak of the growing season in midsummer, and tag them so you remember which ones they are.

283 seed-saving tips

If you want to save leftover seeds or collect seeds from nonhybrid varieties to plant in next year's garden, store them in a cool, dry place. One of the best ways to store seeds is to place the packets in a glass jar with a tight-fitting lid and put the jar in your refrigerator. Put some powdered milk, cornstarch, or silica gel in the jar to absorb any excess moisture. If stored seeds become damp, they will mold and rot.

284 thin fruit for a better harvest

Thin tree fruits (except cherries) to produce a top harvest of larger, better quality fruit. Thin when the fruits are the size of a marble, leaving 3 to 4 inches between apricots or plums, 4 to 5 inches between peaches and nectarines, and 6 to 8 inches between apples and pears.

285 new life for an old stump

When a big old tree has to be cut down, it can be a major project to get the old stump out of the ground. To save a lot of aggravation and work, and to avoid digging up a sizable chunk of your yard, hollow out the center of the stump, fill it with potting mix, and plant some annuals in it.

286 dividing perennials

A rule of thumb for when to divide crowded clumps of perennials:

Divide spring-blooming plants in early fall; divide summer-blooming plants in late fall; divide fall-blooming plants early the following spring.

Most perennials will tolerate division at other times as well, as long as you do not disturb them in winter or during the height of summer.

287 maintaining a vine-covered wall

If you have a clinging vine, such as Boston ivy, growing on a wall that needs repairing or painting, it can be difficult to pull the vine away from the wall without breaking a lot of stems. A better solution is to cut the vine back to the ground in early spring. Let new stems grow and trail along the ground; then fasten them to the wall when the work is finished.

288 hide old woody vines

Tall-growing woody vines tend to develop most of their leaves at the tips of the stems; in older plants, this puts most of the foliage high off the ground and leaves long, bare stems at eye level. Camouflage the lower stems by bending down a flexible, leafy shoot and wrapping it around the bare stem.

289 more flowers for vines

To get more flowers on vines, try training them to grow horizontally instead of vertically.

290 getting wisteria to bloom

If your wisteria fails to bloom, it may be because the soil is too rich. Cut back on fertilizer—especially nitrogen—to encourage the plants to bloom the following year. Other factors that may prevent bloom: The plant isn't getting enough sun, cold winter weather has killed the flower buds, or there is too much top growth in relation to the roots.

291 postponing bolting

To keep lettuce, spinach, mustard, arugula, and other leafy greens from bolting to seed in summer heat, give them some shade. If you cannot plant them in a location that receives some shade in the afternoon, cover them with cheesecloth or shade netting during the hottest part of the day, or set up snow fencing near them to cast shadows on the plants in the afternoon. Giving the plants plenty of moisture will also help postpone bolting, but don't overwater; the soil should be evenly moist but not soggy.

292 cultivate! culti-vate! cultivate!

Frequent cultivation is one of the best ways to have a healthy garden. If you cultivate once a week with a hoe or other cultivating tool, you will keep the soil loose and well aerated and get rid of weeds while they are still small.

293 control daffodil foliage

To keep daffodil foliage looking neat while it develops and matures, braid the leaves together or gather them into bunches and secure with twine or rubber bands. If left alone, the leaves will grow long and floppy and will make the garden look messy until they yellow and can be removed.

294 a simple weed killer

An easy way to get rid of weeds growing in the cracks of a brick patio is to pour liquid chlorine bleach on them.

295 getting rid of poison ivy

Poison ivy, recognized by its clusters of three shiny leaves, is a most obnoxious vine. If it is growing in an open area, repeated, persistent mowing will usually kill it. The other way to eliminate it is with herbicides applied carefully only to the poison ivy, not to any ornamentals.

296 helping the bees

To help bees pollinate fruit trees, cut stems of fertile flowers from the pollinator tree, put them in a bucket of water, and hang the bucket from a branch of the fruit tree that is to be pollinated. Do this early in the morning, before the bees really become active.

297 natural ant repellents

To keep ants away from your plants, sprinkle a good lay-er of cayenne pepper around the plants under attack, or spray the plants with a pepper-and-water solution. Planting calendulas or pot marigolds, the large marigolds called African or American marigolds, pennyroyal, or lavender will also help to repel ants.

298 aphid control

Here is a homemade spray to get rid of aphids: Prepare a solution of soapy water (use a nondetergent soap, like Ivory Snow). Spray the bugs until they are quite wet, and repeat the spraying twice a day until the aphids are gone.

299 earwig traps

Earwigs can do serious damage in gardens where they are abundant. They chew holes in leaves and flowers and gather inside heads of lettuce. You can trap earwigs in tubular containers. Crumple some paper and stuff it loosely inside cardboard tubes from paper towels or toilet tissue. In the evening, place the tubes on the ground in the garden or tie them to branches or stakes put among the plants. The bugs will go inside the tubes to hide. In the morning, empty the traps and dispose of the bugs.

300 another earwig trap

Here's another way to trap earwigs: Put crumpled paper or loose straw inside empty tin cans or flower pots, and prop each container upside down on a stick in the garden. In the morning, empty the earwigs from their hiding places in the containers.

301 how to beat squash vine borers

Squash vine borers are among the most notorious killers of zucchini plants. The vines will be healthy and productive, then suddenly wilt and die for no apparent reason. Sometimes you can save the plant by slitting open the stems, removing and destroying the grubs, and covering the cut stem with soil. A far easier and more effective tactic is to cover the plants with floating row covers while they are young, to prevent the flies from laying their eggs in the first place.

302 win the battle of the borers

Borers can be a terrible pest for fruit trees and for certain ornamentals, such as white birch. A serious borer infestation will kill the tree, usually from the top down. To prevent borers from laying their eggs around the base of a susceptible tree, scatter mothballs around the trunk, or surround the base of the tree with Tanglefoot or another sticky substance.

303 relocating caterpillars

If you find black-and-yellow striped caterpillars eating your parsley, dill, or carrot foliage, don't kill them; they are larvae of the black swallowtail butterfly. If you can transfer them onto some wild Queen Anne's lace, they will be just as happy, and your garden plants will be spared.

304 mothballs in the garden

Mothballs can be useful in the garden. Push them into the soil around shrubs to keep neighborhood dogs and cats from digging around them. Planted near seed potatoes, mothballs repel slugs and other tuber-eating pests. Moth crystals sprinkled over the soil where you are planting carrot seeds is supposed to keep away carrot flies.

305 getting rid of flies

Various kinds of small flies can plague the garden and annoy you when you're working in it. To repel them, plant artemisias (especially *Artemisia abrotanum*, or southernwood), tansy, and marigolds.

306 traps for whiteflies

The best way to get rid of whiteflies is with sticky yellow traps. Whiteflies are attracted to the color yellow. Paint pieces of wood or heavy cardboard with bright yellow oil-based paint; then coat them with Tangletrap or another sticky substance. Hang the traps among and behind the plants under siege, or attach them to stakes. The flies will stick to the traps. When the traps are full, replace them with new ones.

307 a barrier against slugs

Sprinkle wood ashes, salt, sharp sand, crushed eggshells, or diatomaceous earth around the perimeter of the garden to keep out slugs and snails. Since the rough, abrasive surfaces would damage their soft bodies, they will not cross them. Planting lots of sage and hyssop around the perimeter may also repel them.

308 a slug-repelling mulch

The USDA Agricultural Research Service reported in 1990 that a chemical has been isolated from dead quackgrass (a notorious weed) that kills slugs. The chemical acts as a nerve poison on slugs but does not harm other creatures. Try mulching with quackgrass clippings if you have slug problems.

309 slug-busters

Large numbers of slugs cause a great deal of damage. You can scatter slug pellets through the garden if you don't have pets or small children who play there. But there are two safe homemade controls:
● Sink empty tuna cans into the ground up to their tops, and fill them with stale beer. Empty the cans

in the morning and refill them at nightfall.
- Go out into the garden at night with a flashlight and sprinkle salt directly onto any slugs you see.

310 more on slugs

Another way to trap slugs is to lay some lettuce leaves or other large leaves, such as those of rhubarb, in the garden near the plants to attract the slugs. Go out with a flashlight at night or early in the morning, and collect the slugs. Dispose of them in a can of saltwater or tap water with kerosene floated on top.

311 bird control

Birds can be a big help in garden pest-control efforts, but they like to eat some kinds of newly sown seeds and may also attack tiny new plants. To keep them from damaging the garden, interplant with garlic, which the birds don't like. Pull the garlic plants when the other seedlings are 4 to 6 inches tall. You can also put wooden stakes in a random arrangement around the newly planted area, and criss-cross strings among them. Or try hanging aluminum pie pans or strips of foil around the seedbed, or sticking a bunch of toy pinwheels in the soil. Birds are frightened by reflecting light and movement.

312 lavender for the birds

Lavender repels mosquitoes, and birds don't like it either. If birds attack certain plants in your garden, such as young peas or crocuses, plant lavender around them to keep the birds away.

313 protecting trees from mice

Mice like to eat the bark of young trees in winter. To protect them, wrap the trunk with tree wrap, or surround the trunk with a hardware cloth cylinder slightly bigger than the trunk itself, 2 to 3 feet high, and extending 2 inches underground.

314 relief from moles

Moles are repelled by plants in the genus *Euphorbia*, so plant spurge in your garden to keep them away. Dropping mothballs down entrances to their tunnels also helps.

315 plants rabbits hate

To keep rabbits out of the garden, try planting onions, garlic, and foxgloves.

316 harmless rabbit repellents

If rabbits are a problem, sprinkle plants with cayenne pepper, wood ashes, or rock phosphate. Or sprinkle dried blood around young plants. All these materials will have to be reapplied after rain. Another alternative is to bury long-necked bottles of different sizes among or around your plants, leaving the top couple of inches of the necks uncovered. The wind blowing across the bottles creates sounds that frighten rabbits (it works for moles, too).

317 another rabbit repellent

Apparently, rabbits, like most children, don't like liver. You can make a liver spray to keep the bunnies out of your lettuce patch. Soak 4 ounces of fresh beef liver in a gallon of hot water for an hour. Strain, and spray plants with the water. Reapply after rain.

318 sure cure for groundhog trouble

To keep groundhogs out of the garden, set up a wire

fence with 10 extra inches on the bottom. Bend this flap outward, so it faces away from the garden, and cover it with soil. This will provide an effective groundhog barrier. If mice and moles plague your vegetable garden, line the bottom of each bed with hardware cloth.

319 steering deer clear of the garden

Deer are a difficult problem for many suburban gardeners. The only 100% foolproof way to keep them out of the garden is to enclose the entire plot in a "house" of chicken wire or fencing wire, or build a fence at least 9 feet high. If the aesthetics of such a setup don't appeal to you, try one of the commercial deer repellents on the market. Or try hanging bags of human hair (get it from a beauty salon) around the outside of the garden. Deer will pick up the human scent and stay away.

320 disease prevention

The best way to control diseases in the garden is to prevent them in the first place, and the best form of prevention is to practice good sanitation. Remove dropped leaves and plant debris promptly. Keep the garden weeded. Don't work around plants—especially beans—when they are wet. Don't smoke in the garden, particularly around tomatoes, eggplant, and potatoes; if you are a smoker, wash your hands before working in the garden.

321 fighting disease

If a plant becomes diseased, remove the affected parts immediately. If the problem reappears on another part of the plant, pull up the entire plant and dispose of it in the garbage. Do not put diseased plant material on the compost pile. Wash your hands when you finish, and sterilize any tools you used by dipping them in a solution of one part liquid chlorine bleach to nine parts water.

322 dogwood troubles

Flowering dogwoods *(Cornus florida)* are among the loveliest of all spring-blooming trees, but they are currently under attack, both in gardens and in the wild, by a disease known as dogwood anthracnose. If you have established dogwoods, here are some measures you can take to prevent the disease. Keep the trees well maintained: Prune away dead twigs, water during prolonged spells of dry weather, and fertilize once a year. When the leaves come out in spring, spray with a fungicide, and spray two more times at two-week intervals.

If you want to plant new dogwoods, plant Chinese *(Cornus kousa)* dogwoods, which are resistant to the disease (although not immune), until resistant flowering dogwood cultivars are developed.

323 best place for a cold frame

The very best location for a cold frame is next to the south-facing wall of a house, garage, or shed. The frame will be sheltered on the north side, and if the frame is constructed with the back (north) side slightly higher than the front (south) side, the glass top will let in the maximum possible amount of sunlight. If you cannot put the cold frame next to a building, consider piling bales of hay or trash bags full of dry leaves next to the north side to provide some insulation.

324 a cold frame needs fresh air

A cold frame must have ventilation on sunny days to prevent the temperature inside from rising too high, and to let out excess moisture and let in fresh air, which in turn helps prevent mold and mildew from forming. Prop the lid partway open with a stick or block of wood during the sunniest part of the day. If you are away from home all day, you can buy a cold frame with an automatic lid or vent opener.

325 cover a cold frame in winter

During the coldest part of winter, cover a cold frame with old blankets or rugs to insulate it and keep the plants from freezing. Gardeners in the coldest climates may not be able to keep plants going all winter long, but insulating the cold frame can add weeks to the season.

326 how to predict frost

The dates of the first fall and last spring frosts vary from year to year with local weather conditions. If the evening sky is clear and humidity is low, and the air is cool and still, temperatures will drop off rapidly after dark and frost is likely. If the sky is overcast and the air is humid, frost is less likely. Breezy weather also decreases the chance of an early or late frost.

327 plastic tunnels and tents

Use clear polyethylene tunnels and tents to give vegetables a head start in spring. To make a tunnel, stretch the plastic over plastic hoops or make your own hoops from old wire coat hangers. Roll back the plastic on sunny days to allow air circulation. To make a tent, set up a stake on either side of the plants you want to protect. Tie a cord tightly to the stakes, and drape the plastic over the cord. Draw out the sides and weigh down the edges with stones or secure them with pegs. Tunnels work best in row gardens; tents can be used over rows or beds.

Another way to cover a bed is to make a frame of wood lath strips and staple the plastic to the frame. Cut slits in the sides for ventilation

328 homemade hot caps

Hot caps can be placed over individual plants to protect them from unseasonably late frosts in spring or the first frosts in fall. You can buy hot caps made of heavy waxed paper, or you can make your own. Cut the bottom out of gallon-size plastic milk or spring-water jugs, and remove the caps for ventilation. Or cut the bottoms off cardboard milk cartons and open the tops to let in air. (Wash all containers before using them as caps.)

329 protection for bigger plants

Hot caps and other plant protectors are invaluable in northern gardens for getting a jump on the growing season, especially for warmth-loving plants like tomatoes. When it's time for the hot caps to come off, you can stack some old tires around individual plants to protect them from chilly spring winds. Or use cylinders made of heavy plastic.

330 shelter for a cold night

If you can save tomatoes and other tender crops from early frost, you can usually extend the harvest by an extra few weeks. If you expect frost, cover the plants with plastic at night, or make an emergency shelter. Stack bales of hay around the plants and cover with old storm windows to make a temporary cold frame.

331 plant heaters

One way to protect young seedlings or a few treasured plants from an unseasonably late or early frost is to make candle heaters. Set votive candles on the ground around your plants. At night, light the candles and place an inverted clay flowerpot over each one. These heaters should create enough warmth to keep the frost away.

332 protecting fruit trees

If you can plant fruit trees only in a cool location, such as the bottom of a hill where cold air collects, or the side of a north-facing slope, the bark of young trees may crack in winter. Paint the trunks with white latex paint to prevent cracking.

333 winter care for potted plants

If you grow hardy trees, shrubs, or perennials in pots that remain outdoors in winter, their roots will need some protection from cold, drying winds. Sink the pots into the garden to their rims over winter, or at least set them behind a wall. Remember, too, that clay pots usually crack in winter, so plants that stay in containers all year round are best potted in plastic.

334 winter care for conifers

It is important for needled evergreen trees and shrubs to have ample supplies of moisture when the weather turns cold in fall. If the soil is dry and the winter is severe, the plants will suffer water stress that will not become apparent until spring, when brown patches will develop. If autumn brings little rain, water your conifers deeply.

5

TOOLS AND EQUIPMENT

335 how to choose a good tool

To choose a durable, well-made spade, shovel, fork, or other tool, examine the connection between the handle and the blade or head. On lesser quality tools, the joint where the two pieces join is wrapped with a piece of metal. A stronger, better connection is made when the head of the tool extends into a socket that fits completely over the end of the handle for a length of 6 inches or so.

336 easy-to-find tools

Are you always losing your trowel and other small tools in the grass when you set them down? If you paint the handles bright orange or yellow, they'll be easy to spot.

337 baby your tools

Pruning shears and other tools will have a longer life if you keep them clean and the blades sharp. Clean tools after you use them, and give the blades a thin coat of light oil; baby oil and cooking oil work just fine. Don't use motor oil; it is harmful to soil microorganisms.

338 how to sharpen tools

At the end of the season, sharpen the cutting edge of spades and shovels with a metal file. Clamp the tool in a vise, hold the file in both hands, and push it across the tapered edge of the tool, sideways and away from you in a smooth stroke. Don't push the file back and forth; push in one direction, repeating the stroke until the tool has a nice, smooth edge.

339 back-saving strategies

If you have back trouble, always use a kneeling bench when working in the garden; don't bend over. When picking up pots and other objects, bend from the knees and keep your back straight; do not lift with your back muscles. Use long-handled tools to eliminate reaching. Use a wheelbarrow or garden cart to move heavy plants and piles of debris. You can also buy a special kind of spade with a spring-driven lever that lifts and dumps the soil, sparing your back muscles.

340 no-bend gardening

If a member of your gardening family is a senior citizen, is wheelchair-bound, or just doesn't like all the bending that goes with gardening, you can construct a no-bend garden. Build waist-high raised beds, or plant the garden in window boxes and hanging baskets.

341 painless gardening

To take the pain out of gardening, be kind to your body. Use a kneeling pad or bench to cushion your knees. Most important of all, get into the gardening routine gradually in spring. Start out by working only an hour a day in the garden until you get back into shape and your muscles get used to the effort.

342 the right rake

Rakes come in a range of sizes. If your garden is small, buy a small rake with sharp teeth. For a large garden, a rake with a wide, heavy head that you can flip over and use to smooth soil will be more useful. If your soil is dense or full of rocks, you will find it easiest to use a rake with widely spaced teeth.

343 a more efficient hoe

A scuffle hoe, whose head is a pivoting open rectangle formed by steel blades, is a work-saver because you push and pull it, removing weeds with each arm motion.

344 long-distance weeder

To get rid of weeds and cultivate around plants in the middle of a wide flower bed, tie or tape a small hand cultivator to the end of a long bamboo pole. This will eliminate the need to walk in the bed and risk trampling plants.

345 better than a 'barrow

A two-wheeled garden cart is an excellent investment for moving piles of garden debris and large numbers of plants. This kind of cart holds more than a wheelbarrow and isn't as likely to tip over.

108

346 automatic watering for seedlings

An easy way to keep containers of germinating seeds and young seedlings evenly moist is to set the containers on capillary matting. Of course, the containers must have drainage holes. The matting comes with a reservoir. Water is conducted from the reservoir to keep the matting constantly moist. All you have to do is keep water in the reservoir.

347 save that hose!

An all too common problem during watering: Pulling too hard on a hose can cause a kink or, even worse, a crack at the coupling that fastens the hose to the faucet. Here's a solution: Tie a piece of clothesline around the spout, and tie the other end to the hose about a foot below the coupling. The rope will keep the hose from kinking or cracking.

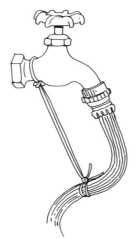

348 electric light for plants

A light garden offers an excellent place to start seedlings indoors. To give plants the red and blue wavelengths they need, use a combination of cool and warm white fluorescent tubes, or cool fluorescents and incandescent bulbs. Wide-spectrum or daylight fluorescent lamps or "grow light" tubes also work well.

349 efficient lighting

For maximum energy efficiency in an indoor light garden, use 4-foot-long, 40-watt fixtures. The ballasts in 4-foot fixtures are more efficient than those in smaller lamps, and 40-watt tubes put out more light per watt than tubes of lower wattage.

350 how much will one light light?

A single fluorescent tube will light an area that is approximately 6 inches wide. A double-tube fixture illuminates an area about 12 inches wide.

351 how close to the light?

The tops of young plants should be 4 inches below fluorescent lights, farther from incandescent bulbs because of the heat. As plants grow taller, they can be 6 to 10 inches below the lights. Keep the lights on twelve to sixteen hours a day.

6

CONTAINERS

352 design tips for container gardens

A well-planned container garden can look every bit as lush and colorful as a garden in the ground. Simply apply the same design principles you use for flower beds and borders. Position plants at several heights by growing tall, medium, and low plants, or by placing the containers on tiered shelving. Suspend plants in hanging baskets above the shelves to add still another dimension. Consider the colors and textures of the plants as well as their relative sizes.

353 group containers together

If you have several plants in small individual pots, group them in a window box, a Victorian fernery, or a wooden tub to create a massed effect. Cover the tops of the pots with moist, unmilled sphagnum moss to conceal them.

354 flower combos for containers

Here are some ideas for annual flowers that make a lovely display planted together in a container:
- Blue-violet salvia and white sweet alyssum surrounded by cascading varieties of petunias in shades of pink, red, and purple.
- Red geraniums, white snapdragons, and white petunias, with red ivy-leaved geraniums cascading over the edge of the container.

- An all-white combination of geraniums and salvia, with ivy-leaved geraniums or sweet alyssum spilling over the edge.
- For cool climates, yellow snapdragons surrounded by blue and yellow pansies, with blue lobelia spilling over the edge of the pot.
- For a hot climate, ornamental peppers with portulaca in brilliant shades of rose, orange, and yellow.

355 three-season window box

To keep your window boxes full of flowers from spring through fall, you can plan three different plantings. Plant in individual pots or plastic window box liners, and simply move the seasonal plants into and out of the window boxes. In early spring, show off small bulbs (crocuses, miniature daffodils, squills, snowdrops, grape hyacinths), or plant pansies. In late spring, replace the bulbs with annuals: begonias, impatiens, torenia, lobelia, coleus for boxes in partial shade; zonal and ivy geraniums, petunias, marigolds, sweet alyssum, and nasturtiums for sunny locations. Plant variegated ivy or vines to trail over the sides and front of the boxes. For fall, replace the annuals with chrysanthemums.

356 a column of plants

To save space in an outdoor container garden and create an attractive display at the same time, make a columnar container to hold plants vertically. Start with a round base: a plywood circle 1½ to 2 feet in diameter drilled with drainage holes. Cut a length of chicken wire and staple it to the plywood to form a column. Line the inside of the column with a sheet of heavy plastic. Then fill the column with an all-purpose potting mix. Set the base of the column on bricks to allow drainage. To plant, punch a hole in the plastic every few spaces in the chicken-wire grid. Gently insert a seedling through each hole, using your fingers to make planting holes in the soil, and work the soil around the plant roots. Finish by planting the top of the container. Water the garden from the top as needed and set in a sunny spot. Petunias, ivy, geraniums, thyme, leaf lettuce, and parsley are a few plants to consider growing in a vertical garden.

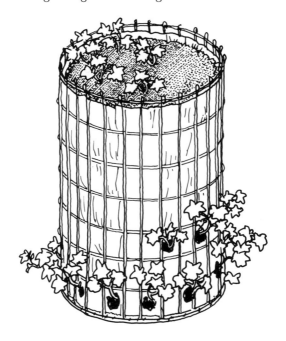

357 a touch of romance

For a romantic-looking container garden or window box, plant lushly with soft colors and graceful forms. Vines climbing a trellis behind containers add height, and trailers dangling from hanging baskets add graceful, active lines that help create a romantic look.

358 a formal window box

To achieve the feeling of stability and repose that is so important to a formal garden, a planting scheme needs balance and control, and plants need to be scrupulously clipped and maintained. This is true whether the design is executed on a grand scale or within the confines of a window box. Design a formal window-box garden on a strong horizontal axis that is broken with equally strong verticals placed at regular intervals. Avoid diagonal lines, which create a feeling of movement, and flowing curves, which encourage the observer's eye to drift from one plant to another. Horizontal and vertical lines in counterpoint give the calmness and control that mark the formal style.

359 window box etiquette

If you live in an apartment and have window boxes mounted on a railing above your downstairs neighbor's terrace, mount a piece of rain gutter to the bottom of the window box to divert water from dripping onto your neighbor's balcony.

360 planting a window box

When planting a window box or tub garden, plant the tallest plants first and work out to the edging plants. If you are planting a small shrub or tree for a focal point, plant that first, and then fill in around it with smaller plants. If the container will hold some climbing vines, install the trellis or other support before planting the vines. If the window box will contain summer bulbs and annuals or perennials, plant the bulbs after the other flowers; if you plant the bulbs first you could inadvertently damage them when digging holes for the other plants.

361 deeper is better

In order to accommodate a variety of plants, a window box should be a minimum of 6 inches deep. Boxes 12 inches deep are even better. Buy the deepest window boxes you can find. A box that holds a greater volume of soil dries out less rapidly than a shallow container and can support a greater variety of plants.

362 installing a window box

To anchor a window box on a long windowsill, fasten screw eyes to both ends of the box and to the window frames. Then secure the box using heavy-gauge wire or hooks. If your box is longer than the sill, install by mounting brackets on the bottom front of the box and screwing the brackets right into the wall. For very narrow windowsills, mount window boxes on the wall with brackets fastened to the bottom or back of each box.

363 the depth of the container

If you are unsure what size container a plant needs, choose one that is about one-third as deep as the height of the plant when it is fully grown.

364 leave room for your hands

If you plan to mount a window box directly on a windowsill, the box should be a few inches shorter than the length of the sill, so there is room to put your hands around the ends of the box to install or remove it.

365 a big pot for herbs

Most herbs adapt readily to container culture, as long as the container is big enough for their roots. As a general rule of thumb, allow 6 to 10 inches of soil for each herb plant.

366 grow herbs indoors

Many herbs will do just fine in pots on a sunny windowsill or in a light garden. It is especially nice to be able to pick sprigs of your favorite fresh herbs in winter. Herbs to grow indoors include small-leaved basils, chervil, chives, dill, fennel, sweet marjoram, mints, oregano, parsley, and thymes.

367 bigger is better

Large containers are better than small ones for most plants growing outdoors in summer. In a large pot, plant roots have more room, and the soil doesn't dry out as fast as in a small pot. Plants in containers need constant watering, which is hard on the soil and leaches nutrients rapidly. Use a rich potting mix with lots of organic matter, and fertilize regularly.

368 moving big containers

To move a tree or shrub in a large pot or tub, a wheeled dolly is ideal. If you haven't got one, you can wedge the blade of a shovel under the pot, tilt the pot and lay it on top of the shovel (this works best on a smooth surface like a patio). Or try maneuvering the pot onto the center of an old rug or blanket and pulling the material to drag the pot.

369 peas and beans in tubs

To grow beans and peas in a tub, put a sturdy pole in the center of the tub. Run strings or wires from the top of the pole to the edges of the tub, like a teepee. Fasten the strings to the edge of the tub by drilling holes and inserting hooks, or by wrapping the string around a nail. The vines will climb the strings.

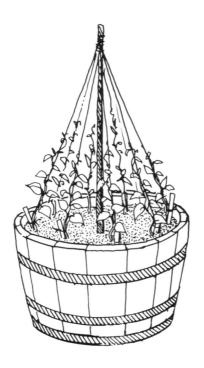

370 disinfecting used pots

If you want to reuse a clay pot, especially one that contained a plant that was diseased, scrub it out with soapy water, rinse, and then disinfect it. Soak the pot for several hours in a solution of one part liquid chlorine bleach to nine parts water. Then rinse thoroughly, and pat dry.

371 styrofoam peanuts

To improve drainage in large pots, tubs, and barrels, put in the bottom of the container about 2 inches of the styrofoam "peanuts" used to pack items for shipping. Then fill with the potting mix of your choice.

372 perfect potting mix

A good growing mix for outdoor container plants combines soil, organic matter, and a lightening agent to add porosity to the medium and insure good drainage. One good all-purpose mixture is three parts potting or garden soil; two parts crumbled compost, leaf mold, or peat moss; and one part perlite, vermiculite, or sharp builder's sand. Blend the ingredients thoroughly, and moisten the potting mix before planting.

373 all-purpose potting mixes

Here are two recipes for all-purpose potting mixes suitable for a wide variety of indoor plants. One mix contains one part soil, one part sharp builder's sand, and one part peat moss, plus 1 tablespoon of bonemeal per quart of mix. Another formula is two parts soil, one part crumbled compost, and one part sand, perlite, or vermiculite. Use whichever is more convenient for you.

374 rich potting mix

Here's a nutrient-rich potting mix that is high in organic matter and recommended for heavy feeders and plants that like lots of humus: one part soil, two parts compost, and one part sharp builder's sand, perlite, or vermiculite.

375 soilless potting mix

This potting mix is lightweight, is made of sterile ingredients, and holds moisture well. It is ideal for rooftop and balcony gardens, where a lightweight potting mix is important, and it is also good for starting seeds. Combine three parts peat moss with one part sharp builder's sand, perlite, or vermiculite. Unless you are using the mix to grow azaleas, blueberries, or other acid-loving plants, add ¾ cup of horticultural lime to each bushel of potting mix to neutralize the acidity of the peat.

376 pasteurizing potting mixes

It is important to pasteurize potting mixes to kill pathogens that could harm seedlings. Here's the classic method. Spread the mix in a disposable aluminum baking pan. Add about a cup of water to moisten; the mix should be damp but not soggy. Put the pan in a turkey-roasting bag or cover it with foil. Heat in a low oven until a meat thermometer inserted in the middle of the pan registers 175 degrees Fahrenheit. Keep the oven at that temperature for a half hour; do not let the temperature go above 180 degrees Fahrenheit.

377 an easier way to pasteurize

An easier way to pasteurize soil is to pour boiling water over the soil in a pan, cover with plastic to hold in the steam, and let sit until the soil is cool.

378 feeding potted plants

Container plants need frequent feeding to replace nutrients leached from the soil by frequent waterings. Water-soluble fertilizers that release their nutrients quickly are best for plants in pots and window boxes. After dilution in water, these fertilizers are either sprayed onto leaves or watered into the soil. Fertilizers directed to the root zone last longer than those applied to leaves and may be given less often—perhaps monthly instead of biweekly.

379 organic liquid fertilizers

Liquid fertilizers are handy for feeding plants in containers. If you garden organically, you can use manure or compost "tea" or fish emulsion and seaweed products for liquid fertilization.

380 a richer diet for potted-up plants

Garden plants potted up and moved indoors for winter often benefit from higher nutrient fertilizers or more frequent feeding than they received outdoors. But be sure to give the plants lots of light so they can make use of the nutrients.

381 tender plants in the north

Northern gardeners can enjoy cold-sensitive shrubs and trees like rosemary and dwarf orange trees by growing them in large tubs that stay outdoors in summer (to dress up a patio, deck, or terrace) and indoors in winter. Mounting the tubs on wheeled dollies or attaching casters to the bottoms of the tub makes the seasonal moving much easier. Casters are sold at most hardware or used-furniture stores.

382 more light for patio plants

To help vegetables and other sun-loving plants get more sun, create reflected light. Set containers next to a white or light-colored wall. Or else paint a sheet of plywood white, or cover it with aluminum foil, and place it behind the plants, or on their east side. A reflector underneath the pots will bounce light as well.

383 mulch for containers

Mulch can help slow the evaporation of moisture in containers just as it does for gardens in the ground. Mulch plants in containers just as you do the main garden, but use fine-textured materials like shredded leaves or cocoa bean hulls. You will still have to water the containers often, but the plants will be better able to make it through a hot day.

384 watering small containers

Watering plants in hanging baskets and other small containers can be a demanding task in hot summer weather, when the heat evaporates the moisture quickly. If you are away at work all day, plants watered in the morning may be limp by late afternoon. To help plants in small pots get through a searing hot day, water in the morning; then place a few ice cubes on top of the soil in each pot.

385 symptoms of overwatering

Although containers outdoors need frequent watering, it is easy to overwater them. During rainy or simply cloudy and humid weather, container plants need less water than during spells of hot, dry, clear weather. When many of a plant's leaves turn yellow and fall off, the plant is probably getting too much water. When soil is constantly wet and soggy, roots can literally suffocate from lack of oxygen. Wet soil also invites disease.

386 watering container vegetables

Water vegetables in containers every day if needed during hot, dry weather. In warm climates, you may have to water twice a day. Feed the plants once a week with an all-purpose liquid fertilizer or seaweed concentrate or fish emulsion.

387 extending moisture

If you are going away for a day or two in summer, here's a way to keep plants in small pots from drying out. Group small pots in a large tub or window box, filling in around them with soil, sand, or vermiculite. Water the pots and the material between them thoroughly, and they will hold the moisture longer than they would individually.

388 longer season for tender plants

To extend the growing season of tender plants in a cold climate, plant them in pots and set the containers in front of a south-facing masonry or stucco wall that is white or light-colored. Additional warmth from the sun will bounce off the wall and onto the plants.

389 summer vacation for houseplants

Many houseplants enjoy spending summer outdoors in a partly shaded location. To cut down on watering, you can sink plants in clay pots into the garden. To prevent potted plants from rooting into the soil, give the pots a sharp twist once a month to break off any new roots that may have escaped through the drainage holes.

7

LAWNS

390 reducing lawn maintenance

A lawn requires more maintenance than just about any other part of a garden. To cut down on the amount of work, consider replacing part of your lawn with groundcovers. It also helps to choose your grass carefully. Pick a species that is adapted to your part of the country, to the sun or shade conditions in your yard, and to your soil type.

391 easy-mow lawn

A lawn that is rounded in shape is easier to mow, water, and keep neat than strict square or rectangular shapes with straight edges and sharp corners.

392 small lawn, low maintenance

To cut down on the time and effort required to keep up a lawn, design the lawn to be only as big as you really need it to be. For example, if you want to use the lawn for outdoor dining or sitting, it can cover a relatively small area. Use groundcover or attractive paving in other parts of your yard.

393 drought-tolerant lawn

In a dry location, plant a lawn that contains perennial ryegrass, fine fescues, and tall fescues, and water it only when necessary.

394 edge the lawn

To keep the lawn from creeping into the garden, edge it. You can do this in one of several ways: Use a tool that slices into the sod and severs the roots, or bury bricks lengthwise, with just an inch or so of each brick above ground, to form a barrier. You can also use edging strips, although because they are thin the grass may grow right over them.

395 eliminating thatch

Thatch is the buildup of undecomposed plant debris at the base of grass plants. Contrary to popular opinion, it is not caused by clippings left by the lawn mower. The best means of permanently eliminating thatch is to have plenty of earthworms in your soil. But to encourage earthworms to live under your lawn, avoid chemicals. Chemically treated lawns repel birds, too.

396 watering the lawn

When you water the lawn, water until the soil is moist 4 to 6 inches deep. Frequent light waterings will produce shallow-rooted grass plants that will suffer during dry weather and may burn in the hot sun. If possible, water in the morning or early evening; at midday a significant portion of the water will evaporate before it reaches the roots, especially if you are using an overhead sprinkler.

397 another use for sod

Sod removed to establish new garden beds can repair damaged areas of your lawn. Remove the old grass in spots where it is thin or unhealthy. Work some compost into the soil; then lay down a new piece of healthy sod, cut to fit the space. Press the sod in place, and water regularly until it establishes new roots and starts to grow.

398 keeping birds off seeded lawns

Birds love grass seed. To keep them away from newly seeded lawns, cover the seeds with straw or hay. The mulch will also keep the seeds from washing away in the rain and will help keep the soil moist. Leave the mulch in place until shoots appear.

399 keep those clippings

If you mow the lawn frequently—that is, before the grass grows more than a third taller than you want it—you can leave the clippings where they fall. As they decompose, they will add organic matter and nutrients to the soil. Contrary to popular opinion, clippings left in the grass do not cause thatch.

400 don't mow when wet

Do not mow the lawn when the grass is wet; the clippings will stick together in wet clumps that can rot and become slimy and smelly. They will also clog the mower and rust the blade.

401 dull blades don't cut it

It is important to keep lawn mower blades sharp; dull blades do not cut cleanly but rip and shred the grass, leaving unkempt, ragged edges that are more susceptible to damage from pests and diseases.

402 don't cut it too close

Don't mow your lawn too short. Longer leaves will shade the roots, and the plants will not dry out as fast. Taller plants also develop deeper roots that will be better able to withstand drought and fend off weeds. Do not mow shorter than 2½ inches, especially in summer.

403 making mowing easier

To reduce mowing chores, turn isolated groups of trees into tree islands, joining them with mulch or a ground-cover instead of lawn. If you have a birdbath or lawn ornaments, set them in a patch of groundcover instead of lawn, so you don't have to mow around them.

404 liming and fertilizing

If you put both lime and fertilizer on your lawn, don't apply them at the same time or they may bind each other up and prove useless to the lawn. Fertilize in early spring, early summer, and early fall with a slow-release formula. Apply lime anytime, but not when you're fertilizing.

405 an even spread

If you use chemical fertilizers on your lawn, be careful to spread them evenly over the grass. An overconcentration of fertilizer will leave burn spots, while areas of the lawn that get no fertilizer will become chlorotic (yellow).

406 chemical-free nematode control

Seaweed meal often works better than chemical nematicides to control nematodes in a lawn, and it also helps plants resist fungus diseases. You will need 62½ pounds of meal for a ¼-acre lawn.

407 easy care for slopes

On a bank or slope that is difficult to mow, plant a groundcover instead of grass to virtually eliminate maintenance. Try vinca, ajuga, lamium, or for shade, epimedium, European wild ginger *(Asarum europaeum)*, pachysandra, or violets. Or try a prostrate form of juniper or cotoneaster.

408 a composition of groundcovers

In a garden where trees and shrubs, rather than flower beds, are the main feature, you can add interest with a colorful composition of groundcovers. Consider planting broad drifts of euonymus or ivy with different variegation patterns, or contrast the electric blue flowers of ceratostigma against a golden-leaved thyme or hosta or the pink flowers of Lancaster geranium. Or try a polka-dot duo of pulmonaria and hypoestes.

409 groundcover textures

The leaf texture of groundcover plants can affect the quality of light in their immediate vicinity. Narrow-leaved plants such as lawn grasses absorb light and can tone down a very bright area. Broad-leaved groundcovers such as ajuga and European wild ginger reflect light and can brighten a dull corner of the garden.

127

410 establishing groundcovers

Most groundcovers take a couple of years to spread out enough to carpet an area. In the meantime, weeds will grow in the bare areas between plants. The usual approach to keeping down weeds is to pull them or to apply a preemergent herbicide. For a more interesting approach, interplant vegetables, herbs, or annual flowers among the groundcover plants to form a living mulch that will keep down weeds until the groundcover fills in.

411 groundcovers for small spaces

If your landscape is small, such as a city courtyard, plant small-leaved groundcovers like vinca, creeping thyme, miniature euonymus or Corsican mint. Larger-leaved plants such as pachysandra and European wild ginger may appear out of scale.

412 just one is enough

In a small garden or a flower garden, it is best to plant just one kind of groundcover in any given area. A patchwork of several different types will not produce the unifying effect that is a groundcover's purpose.

413 connect with groundcovers

Use a groundcover to blend and unify different elements of a landscape into a coherent garden. A groundcover is an elegant way to tie beds and borders to one another. It can also bring a sense of coherence to a variety of specimen shrubs and trees in different shapes and sizes, and connect groups of trees and shrubs to the ground.

414 carpeting shady areas

Even a shade-tolerant lawn grass will not grow well under the shade of large old trees with dense canopies and shallow roots, such as Norway maples. Try removing some of the lower branches from the trees to admit more light. Shade-tolerant groundcovers include European wild ginger, lily of the valley, epimedium, English ivy, bishop's weed, lamium, pachysandra, or pulmonaria.

415 propagating pachysandra

If you grow pachysandra as a groundcover and would like to start a new patch in another part of your property, there's no need to buy new plants. In late spring or early summer, trim the plants you already have. Set the stems of the trimmings in a container of equal parts sand and peat moss or peat and vermiculite. Keep the medium moist and the cuttings will root and be ready to plant in a few weeks.

416 grasses in problem places

Many ornamental grasses have spreading root systems that can help open up dense soil. They also work well to stabilize a slope where erosion is a problem. Ornamental grasses are easy to grow, are tolerant of many types of soil, and are seldom bothered by pests and diseases.

417 a boundary of ornamental grasses

Plant tall ornamental grasses along the periphery of your property for a low-maintenance privacy screen and noise buffer. The grasses make a soothing sound when they sway in the breeze, and if you let them stand in winter, they add soft golden or silvery tones and sculptural shapes to the landscape.

8

FLOWERS

418 perennials for shade

Quite a number of perennials are suited to a lightly shaded garden. Some of the prettiest perennials for shade include bergenia, tiarella, hosta, monkshood, Japanese anemone, columbine, goatsbeard, astilbe, brunnera, campanula, bleeding heart, plumbago, lily of the valley, epimedium, filipendula, hardy geranium, golden star, crested iris, cardinal flower, beebalm, forget-me-not, wild blue phlox, creeping blue phlox, trollius, and violet.

419 annuals for shade

Most gardeners are familiar with the big three annual shade plants: impatiens, wax begonias, and coleus. But many other annuals also bloom happily in light shade, including balsam, browallia, English daisy, lobelia, lunaria, forget-me-not, sweet alyssum, thunbergia, and torenia.

420 enjoy a bit of summer in winter

To grow flowers indoors in winter, take cuttings from garden annuals (geraniums, wax begonias, impatiens) in late summer. Cut off the tip of the plant on a slant, right above the second set of leaves from the top. Stick the stem of the cutting in a pot or flat of moist rooting medium, and enclose the container in a plastic bag to keep humidity high. Keep the container out of direct sun, and support the plastic with popsicle sticks or bent coat hangers to keep it from touching plant leaves. Water (from below) as needed to keep soil moist. Remove the plastic when roots have formed (a gentle tug on the stem will meet with resistance). Move the plant to a sunny windowsill or a light garden.

421 flowers by use

The greatest variety in a flower garden is possible with a combination of annuals, perennials, bulbs, and flowering shrubs. But a garden containing all these kinds of flowers is complicated to plan and maintain. If you are not yet ready for such a project, decide what use is most important and plant accordingly. If cut flowers are the goal, grow long-stemmed annuals, bulbs, and perennials well suited to the purpose. If you want dried flowers, plant everlastings and other flowers that dry well.

422 spring flowers

For the earliest possible spring flowers, each fall plant early-blooming bulbs such as crocuses and snowdrops in the warmest areas on your property. How do you find the warmest places? Look for where the snow melts first in winter. One likely spot is next to the south-facing wall of a house.

423 a special flower for dry soil

Portulaca (rose moss) blooms happily in poor, dry soil as long as it has plenty of sun. The plant also self-sows and will come back year after year. Portulaca's low-growing, brilliantly colored flowers are delightful bordering a sidewalk or driveway, on top of a stone wall, between paving stones, and in a rock garden.

424 more drought-tolerant annuals

If you live in a dry climate or want to plant annuals in

window boxes or small outdoor containers that will dry out quickly in summer, try growing (in addition to portulaca) African daisy, sweet alyssum, celosia, globe amaranth, xeranthemum, marigold, nasturtium, salvia, and strawflower.

425 perennials for dry places

If you want a perennial garden and live in a dry climate or seashore area, plant achillea, artemisia, coreopsis, daylily, euphorbia, butterfly weed, sedum, lavender, rudbeckia, and santolina.

426 quick color in a meadow

Meadow gardens usually take two or three years to become established and start blooming. To have color the first year, mix some annual seeds into the meadow mix before you sow. Some good annuals to grow in a meadow are bachelor's button, annual coreopsis or calliopsis, California poppy, and cosmos.

427 adapting plants to dry soil

Some plants that ordinarily grow best in full sun where soil is rich and moist will cope better with dry soil if given some shade during the day. Perennials that behave this way include lady's mantle, Japanese anemone, bergenia, purple coneflower, peach-leaved bellflower, snakeroot, cranesbills, daylilies, coral bells, loosestrife, and meadow rue.

428 try some exotic bulbs

Calla lilies are among the most exotically beautiful flowering bulbs. Although they are not hardy except in warm climates, you can plant them outdoors in spring and dig them up in fall to store indoors over winter. Calla lilies will also grow in water and make a stunning addition to a water garden when planted in a container of soil set in a pool or pond.

429 know your sources

Buy bulbs, wildflowers, and native plants only from a source that will guarantee that the plants were nursery-propagated and not collected from the wild. Some bulbs are actually endangered in the wild as a result of overcollection in their native countries, such as Turkey. Beware of bulbs and native plants at unusually low prices; if they sound too good to be true, they probably are.

430 a flashy begonia for shade

The tuberous begonia is an easy-to-grow bulb that is too often overlooked. Tuberous begonias produce big flowers in a host of hot colors that make a welcome change from the usual wax begonias and impatiens in a shady garden. The bulbs are tender, so plant them when the soil warms in spring and dig them up in fall.

431 the biggest mums

For super chrysanthemums, pinch back the plants to encourage bushiness, and disbud them to get bigger flowers. To disbud, remove all but one bud from each shoot. Pinch back the plants in early summer and again a month later. Don't pinch after mid-July, or the plants may not bloom before heavy frost kills them, especially in northern gardens.

432 don't blame goldenrod

Goldenrods are lovely additions to wildflower gardens and naturalistic landscapes. If you shy away from planting goldenrod because you're afraid it will aggravate your hayfever, stop worrying. Goldenrod does not cause hayfever; the real culprit is ragweed, which often grows near goldenrod in the wild, is less obvious to observers, and flowers at the same time as goldenrod.

433 when peonies don't bloom

If your herbaceous peonies refuse to bloom, they are probably planted too deep. Set new plants at the same depth they were growing in the nursery (look for the soil line on the stem). Dig up reluctant bloomers in fall and replant them with the red growth buds on the crowns 1 to 1½ —no more than 2—inches below the soil surface.

434 deadheading roses

When removing spent flowers from roses, cut the stem back to directly above a leaf made up of five leaflets. Many roses will rebloom if pruned this way; the dormant bud will be stimulated into producing a new flowering stem.

435 roses for the seashore

You say you love roses but they won't grow in your garden near the sea? Plant rugosa roses. The spiny bushes will grow even in a sand dune, and they produce masses of fragrant single flowers in shades of pink and red, as well as white.

436 easy-care roses

If you love roses but not the spraying, pruning, and fussing that goes with them, grow the new landscape roses now on the market. These shrub roses require far less care than hybrid teas, grandifloras, and floribundas and are less troubled by pests and diseases.

Many of them bloom vigorously through much of summer, sometimes continuing until frost.

437 winterizing roses

Bare-root roses are usually best planted in the fall. To help newly planted roses survive their first winter, mound up about 6 inches of soil around the base of the plant for extra insulation. Remove the mounded soil gradually in early spring.

438 longer life for geraniums

The common garden geranium *(Pelargonium × hortorum)* is usually grown as an annual, but it is actually a frost-tender perennial. You can store geraniums over the winter by inducing a state of dormancy. Before the first fall frost, dig the plants (only healthy ones!) from the garden. Bring them into the basement, and let them sit until the soil is completely dry. Brush the soil off the roots, and put each plant in a paper bag. Close the top of the bag with string or a rubber band, and leave the bags in the basement or another cool place with relatively high humidity. Check the plants periodically, and mist with water if the stems become seriously shriveled. In spring, cut back the stems to green tissue, and plant the plants in pots. Keep the soil moist, and when the plants start to grow, move them to a light garden or bright windowsill. Plant outdoors when all danger of frost is past.

439 cutting flowers

If you want to cut some flowers from your garden to bring indoors, take a bucket of lukewarm water out to the garden with you. As soon as you cut each stem, stand it in the water; the less time cut flowers are out of water, the longer they will last. Use lukewarm water because it is easiest for stems to absorb; water that is too hot or too cold can cause shock.

440 longer life for cut flowers

To make cut flowers last longer, remove all leaves that would be underwater in the vase, and change the water in the vase every day or two. Cutting about half an inch off the bottom of each stem when you change the water helps as well.

441 homemade flower desiccant

If you grow flowers for drying, you don't need to purchase expensive silica gel in which to dry them. A half-and-half mixture of borax and cornmeal works just as well and is much cheaper.

9

VEGETABLES

442 big harvest, small garden

To make the most of a small vegetable garden, grow crops that produce the greatest amount of food for the amount of space they take up. Vegetables with the biggest yield per unit of space include bush beans, pole beans, beets, carrots, leaf lettuce, onions, peppers, radishes, spinach, bush-type summer squash, tomatoes, and turnips.

443 easy rotating

Rotate vegetable crops each year to prevent soilborne diseases. Rotation is especially important for members of the cabbage family, which should not be planted in the same spot more than once every three years. The simplest rotation cycle is to plant a leafy crop where a root crop grew before, and then follow the next year with a fruiting crop.

444 efficient design for vegetables

The traditional single-row vegetable garden wastes a lot of space. Instead, try planting in wide rows or in intensive beds.

To plant in wide rows, set plants equidistant from one another in all directions in bands 1½ feet wide; for intensive beds, do the same in squares or rectangles. Space the bands or rectangles 2 to 2½ feet apart, separated by access paths. Although individual plants will produce less than they would in a single-row garden, the total yield per square foot of garden space can be as much as four times greater than in a single-row garden.

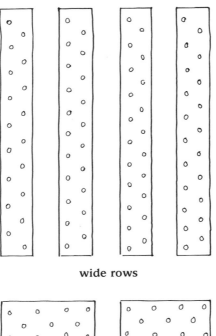

wide rows

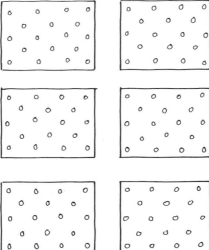

intensive beds

445 rotate to control pests

Rotating crops in a vegetable garden can help thwart insect pests. If an insect lays eggs near a favorite host plant and that plant has been moved to a different part of the garden, when the eggs hatch the new generation of pests may not be able to find their target food source.

446 easy-care vegetables

Low-maintenance vegetables include arugula, asparagus (it takes work to plant but once established needs little care), bush beans, beets, cabbage, carrots, Swiss chard, collards, garden cress, escarole, leaf lettuce, okra, peas, peppers, radishes, spinach, bush summer squash, and determinate varieties of tomatoes.

447 vegetables for shade

The following vegetables will grow in a partially shaded garden that receives two hours of direct sun and indirect light the rest of the day: arugula, beets, broccoli, cabbage, carrots, Chinese cabbage, endive and escarole, garden cress, kale, leaf lettuce, mustard greens, peas, sorrel, spinach, Swiss chard, and turnips.

448 the quickest reward

For an early harvest, grow fast-maturing vegetables such as garden cress, radishes, scallions, leaf lettuce, mustard greens, spinach, and summer squash. Also look for early-maturing varieties of your other favorite vegetables.

449 grow up instead of out

To save space in a small vegetable garden, train vining

crops to grow vertically on a trellis. Beans, peas, cucumbers, squash, and tomatoes can all be trained to grow vertically instead of sprawling over the ground. Support large, heavy fruits such as winter squash and melons with cloth or twine slings looped under the fruit and tied to the trellis. Fasten stems to the support every few inches with loosely tied string, soft yarn, or twist-ties.

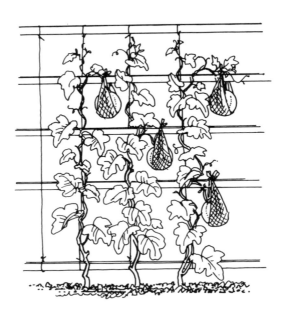

450 the importance of day length

Spinach, onions, and potatoes are especially sensitive to day length (the number of daylight hours in a twenty-four-hour period). Spinach and potatoes tend to bloom when days are long (the main reason spinach bolts to seed in summer); some onions need long days to form bulbs, and other varieties need shorter days. With these vegetables it is important that you plant varieties suited to your geographic location. Buy seeds or sets from local garden centers or mail-order suppliers in your part of the country.

451 no-dig gardening

No-till gardening is a work-saving way to grow vegetables and herbs that is especially valuable for older
gardeners and others who don't like to do a lot of
bending and stooping. For the method to be effective,
you must start with good soil. Then each year at the
end of the growing season, cut the plants down to soil
level. Gather up the plant debris and put it on the compost pile. Leave the roots to rot in the ground, and add
compost or other organic matter to the soil. Another
way to eliminate hard digging is to keep a vegetable or
herb garden permanently mulched with a thick layer
of hay or straw; to plant, just pull aside the mulch and
expose the soil.

452 tender bites

If you grow salad crops—lettuce, cress, arugula, beets,
carrots, and others—you can thin them twice, once
when they are very small and again a few weeks later.
The second group of thinnings make tender, fine-textured additions to salads.

453 maximum yields

To increase a plant's total yield, remove the female
flowers that appear during the first two weeks the
plant blooms. Female flowers have a swelling at the
base that will turn into a fruit after fertilization. The
plants will then be a bit larger and more mature when
they set fruit. The harvest will be later but larger.

454 extending spring harvests

To extend the harvest of spring spinach, lettuce, and
other leafy greens that bolt to seed in hot summer
weather, make sure they have abundant, even moisture, and give them some shade in the afternoon.
Shade netting made of polypropylene works well and

can be purchased from mail-order garden supply
companies. You can also use cheesecloth.

455 another season-extending trick

To extend the harvest of fast-growing vegetables like
radishes, leaf lettuce, and beets, instead of planting
the whole crop at once, make several plantings two to
three weeks apart.

456 a good pair

To save space in a vegetable garden, try planting a late
crop of pole beans next to sunflowers or corn, and letting the bean vines climb their neighbors' tall stems.
The beans will also help fix nitrogen in the soil for the
corn, which needs it.

457 pea-planting pointers

Peas and onions can go into the garden as soon as the
soil is workable. But if the weather is poor, wait a
week or two to plant peas. Although they grow best in
cool weather, peas cannot tolerate severe frost and
prolonged exposure to subfreezing temperatures. If
the soil is too cold when you plant, the seeds will be
very slow to germinate. The plants will grow better if
you wait until conditions are more hospitable.

458 extending summer harvests

If you protect tomatoes, peppers, eggplant, and late
beans from the first light frost or two, you can keep
harvesting during the several weeks of warm Indian
summer weather that usually follow. When frost
threatens, cover the plants at night with plastic,
cloches, hot caps, row covers, hay, or straw—even
with burlap or an old blanket. Remove the covers the
next morning.

459 fall vegetables

Many cool-weather crops that are usually planted in spring are actually easier to grow for fall harvest. Broccoli, spinach, cabbage, beets, carrots, kale, brussels sprouts, leaf lettuce, arugula, cress, and radishes can all be planted in midsummer to mature in the cooler weather of fall. Garden centers do not usually have plants available at this time of year, so plan on starting your fall garden from seed. These cool-weather plants will have better flavor and will be less likely to bolt to seed than those that mature in summer.

460 extending the harvest of greens

To extend the harvest of leafy crops as long as possible in fall, shield the plants from the rays of the morning sun. When a frosty night is followed by a bright, sunny morning, the sun can cause temperatures inside the plant to rise too quickly, and tissues will be damaged by the rapid temperature swings. To protect plants, erect a screen made of burlap or cloth, supported by wooden stakes or a wire frame, on the southeast side of the plants.

461 when frost is a blessing

Some vegetables actually taste better *after* they have been exposed to some light frost. The cold mellows and sweetens their flavor by causing some of the starches in the plants to change to sugars. Brussels sprouts, parsnips, kale, and carrots all taste sweeter after frost.

462 storing crops in the garden

Save space in your refrigerator by storing cold-tolerant root crops right in their garden beds or rows over the winter. Carrots, leeks, turnips, and parsnips can stay in most gardens all winter. Where winters are not too severe, you can also store beets, celeriac, and winter radishes this way. In addition to saving space indoors, in-ground storage also keeps the vegetables in good condition longer than refrigerator storage, because of the moisture in the soil.

In late fall, when the soil surface freezes, mulch the vegetables with 1 to 2 feet of salt hay, shredded dry leaves, or straw. Tuck mulch close around plant stems. Lay boards or evergreen boughs on top to hold the mulch in place. If you think mice may pose problems, cover the mulch with hardware cloth. Mark the location with tall stakes. The mulch will keep the ground from freezing deeply, so you can dig vegetables as needed all winter.

463 don't pick asparagus

When harvesting asparagus, cut the stems at ground level with a sharp knife. Do not pull or snap them off; you could inadvertently damage the plant crowns.

464 growing cucumbers in Vermont

If you live in the North, where the frost-free growing season is short, you may have difficulty growing cucumbers, melons, winter squash, and other crops that need a long, warm growing season. Look for fast-maturing varieties bred for a short growing season, or try starting seeds indoors in late March. However, these crops are all difficult to transplant. To better the odds, start seeds in peat pots or soil blocks so that the roots suffer minimum disturbance during transplanting.

465 the best-tasting melons

Melons need warmth to develop a full flavor. While the fruits are maturing, set them on top of cans or strawberry boxes to raise them off the ground and above the leaves, for maximum sun exposure.

466 ripening melons and squash

Around the end of August (later in warm climates), pick all remaining blossoms and tiny fruits from melon and winter squash vines so the plants can channel their energy into ripening the larger fruits before the first frost.

467 the most peas and beans

To get the maximum harvest from peas and beans, treat the seeds with legume inoculant before sowing. The inoculant is a powder containing bacteria that help the plants fix nitrogen in the soil. You can buy it at garden centers or from mail-order seed companies. To coat the seeds, pour the powder into a paper bag, add the seeds, and shake. Moistening the seeds first helps the powder to adhere better.

468 a second harvest of scallions

If you like scallions, here's a way to grow a quick second crop. When you pull green onions from the garden, remove the thin outer skin, and cut off a ½-inch section of the root tip. Replant the root tip immediately, about an inch deep. Handle carefully to avoid damaging the root tendrils. You'll have a new crop of scallions in six to eight weeks.

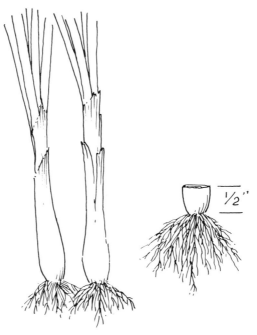

469 flavorful tomatoes

The taste of a tomato depends on a combination of acids, sugars, and volatile compounds. The amount of sun a tomato plant gets affects the development of its flavor. If conditions are rainy or shady, tomatoes won't taste as good as they could. A plant that has more leaf area per fruit passes more of the flavor compounds into each fruit. For the best flavor, do not prune nonfruiting suckers from the plants, and give them all the sun you can.

470 herbs for shady gardens

A number of herbs will grow happily in partial shade, where they get two hours of direct sun daily and indirect light the rest of the day. Shade-tolerant herbs include chervil, chives, mints, and parsley.

471 don't kill herbs with kindness

Herbs grow best when you don't fuss over them. It is essential *not* to overfertilize or overwater herbs. It is better to give them too little attention than too much.

472 low-maintenance herbs

Low-maintenance plants for herb gardens include bee-balm, chervil, chives, dill, fennel, nasturtiums, parsley and sweet violets.

473 harvesting herbs

The best time to harvest herbs for drying is on a cool, sunny morning, after the dew dries from the leaves but before the hottest part of the day. Herbs get their flavor and scent from volatile oils in their tissues. In the late morning, these oils reach their peak concentration. The heat of the afternoon sun draws some of the oils out of the leaves.

474 freeze herbs for better flavor

To preserve more of the flavor of fresh herbs, freeze them rather than dry them. Remove large leaves from stems; small-leaved, thin-stemmed herbs like thyme are better frozen on the stem. Put in air-tight freezer containers or sealable plastic bags, seal the container, and freeze. Chervil, dill, chives, parsley, and basil are especially good frozen.

475 an easy way to dry herbs

The traditional way to dry herbs for long-term storage is to hang them upside down in bunches to air-dry, but it is faster and easier to dry them in a microwave oven. Separate the leaves from the stems, and spread them on a double layer of paper towels. Put them in the microwave on high for two minutes. Stir the leaves, and microwave two more minutes. If the leaves are not yet completely dry, stir and microwave for another two minutes. The leaves should be dry enough to be easily broken but not so dry that they crumble into powder at a touch.

476 how to dry herb seeds

To dry seed heads of herbs such as dill, fennel, caraway, and coriander, cut them with long stems attached when the seeds darken in color but before they drop. Gather several stems in a bunch, and put them in a paper bag with the seed heads pointing toward the bottom of the bag. Tie the top of the bag shut with string, and hang in a well-ventilated place. The seeds will fall to the bottom of the bag when they are dry.

10

TREES AND SHRUBS

477 best time to plant trees

Many trees can be planted in either spring or fall, but some trees should be planted only in spring because they take a long time to establish themselves in the soil after planting. Trees that should be planted only in spring include magnolias, most types of oak, golden-rain tree, tulip tree, tupelo, and Japanese zelkova.

478 low-maintenance trees and shrubs

If you have little time for landscaping chores, plant trees and shrubs that need little maintenance. Good trees include hedge maple, river birch, European horn-beam, saucer magnolia, Chinese elm, and Japanese zelkova.

For low-maintenance shrubs, consider forsythia, witch hazel, holly, bayberry, spiraea, and viburnum.

479 good as gold

Golden-leaved and variegated trees and shrubs make handsome focal points in a home landscape, but many of them tend to scorch in hot sun. Some that will hold up in heat and bright light are a golden-leaved tulip tree (*Liriodendron tulipifera* 'Aureo-marginatum') *Spiraea ×bumalda* 'Monhub', and the gold coast juniper (*Juniperus chinensis* 'Aurea').

480 for the birds

If you want to attract birds to your property, plant trees and shrubs that offer food and nesting places. Trees include dogwood, holly, cedar, pine, birch, oak, crabapple, mountain ash, hackberry, hawthorn, and alder trees. Good shrubs for birds include autumn olive, rockspray cotoneaster, Japanese barberry, bayberry, pyracantha, and rugosa rose. If you want vines, plant American bittersweet, a non-invasive species of honeysuckle, Boston ivy, or Virginia creeper.

481 eliminate suckers

If you grow grafted roses or fruit trees, watch for suckers growing around the base of the plant and remove them whenever you spot them. These suckers grow from the rootstock; if allowed to grow, they will eventually overwhelm the less vigorous scion (top growth), and you will be left with a plant like the less desirable rootstock parent.

482 decreasing summer stress

It is best *not* to plant young trees (or other plants) in summer, when growing conditions are stressful. If you must plant a tree in summer, snip off the leaves after planting to induce an artificial state of dormancy. Use a scissors and snip off leaves at the petiole, leaving part of the petiole on the tree. The tree will be less likely to dehydrate, and will send new roots out into the soil. Eventually new leaf buds will grow from the old leaf bases.

483 low-water trees and shrubs

These days we must all be mindful of our gardens' water requirements. Trees and shrubs that tolerate drought include tatarian maple, golden-rain tree, Japanese pagoda tree, Colorado blue spruce, hackberry, barberry, flowering quince, broom, honeysuckle, and cotoneaster.

484 critical watering

Most trees and shrubs can withstand a certain amount of dry weather. But in late summer, if the weather is dry, many trees and shrubs will suffer without water. This is the time of year when the plants are setting buds for next spring's flowers and leaves.

485 shade in the city

Tough trees that can tolerate the difficult growing conditions in urban areas (poor soil, low light, little water, pollution) include ginkgo, Colorado spruce, star magnolia, Bradford pear, and yew.

486 preparing to plant a tree

When planning where trees will go, allow enough space for each tree to reach its full mature size.

Improve the soil to a depth of a foot or so over an area five times the diameter of the tree's rootball. This makes it easy for roots to grow out into the soil.

487 tree planting tips

When planting a tree, do not compact the soil around the roots by stepping on it. Instead, set the tree in the hole and fill the hole halfway with soil; then water to settle the soil around the roots. Fill the hole with soil, and water again.

Plant so the top of the rootball is even with the surrounding soil.

488 plant trees to save energy

Plant trees on the southeast or southwest side of your

house to help keep the house cooler in summer and to cut air-conditioning expenses. Plant a row of evergreens or other trees on the north side of the house to serve as a buffer against icy winter winds and to lower heating bills.

489 get rid of unwanted shoots

Remove promptly any suckers or water sprouts that develop on your fruit trees. Suckers are shoots growing from the roots around the base of the tree. Water sprouts are weak vertical shoots that grow from older branches and often appear after the tree has been severely pruned. Both types of growth sap strength from the tree, and neither will produce fruit.

490 getting reluctant trees to bear

If a young fruit tree won't bear although it is old enough to do so, first test the soil. If no nutrient deficiencies exist, try spreading the branches to force them close to a 45-degree angle from the trunk. You can use branch spreaders or tie down the branches with heavy wire or strong ropes fastened to stakes in the ground. Thread wire through a piece of rubber hose where the wire touches the branches, to avoid injuring the tree.

491 urban elegance

For an elegant, low-maintenance garden in a city backyard or other tiny plot, plant dwarf conifers. There are dwarf firs, junipers, cypresses, spruces, pines, cedars, and other trees in a variety of shapes from columnar to round to weeping to prostrate, as well as a surprising range of colors, including gray-green, blue-green, golden, silvery, bronze, and purplish. Dwarf conifers generally need little care and look good all year.

492 help for elongated conifers

Sometimes a needled evergreen will develop a leader that is too long; as a result, the lateral branches are far apart on the trunk, with bare stretches of trunk between them. To shorten the bare spaces, prune back the leader by half. Make the cut in spring, when new growth occurs and the new shoot is still fairly young. If the shoot is too old when cut, a new growth bud will not form, and the tree will stop growing.

493 a new leader to follow

If the leader of an upright conifer breaks off from storm damage or some other cause, you can train a side shoot to take its place. In spring, when the wood is flexible, bend a lateral shoot at the top of the tree into a vertical position. Hold it in place with a wooden brace made from a long dowel; fasten the shoot to the brace with soft yarn or cloth tied in a figure eight. Leave the brace in place at least until autumn.

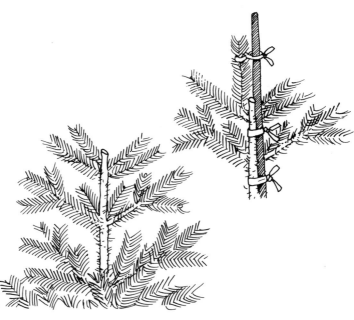

494 instant shrubs

To get the look of a shrub in a single growing season, plant castor bean or summer cypress, both fast-growing annual foliage plants.

495 fragrance from shrubs

Fragrance can come from easy-care shrubs as well as from a flower garden. Shrubs with fragrant flowers include summersweet, lilac, fothergilla, honeysuckle, Carolina allspice, jasmine, daphne, and Virginia sweetspire.

496 shrubs for shade

Shrubs that grow in shade include Hinoki false cypress, summersweet, wintercreeper, oakleaf hydrangea, Japanese holly, Japanese kerria, rhododendron, jetbead, and yews.

497 the earliest flowers

For fragrant flowers outdoors in February or March, plant witch hazel. The ribbony yellow or copper-colored blossoms are among the very earliest in the garden, opening when the rest of the landscape is still gray and drab.

498 deadheading lilacs

Lilacs bloom best when the dead flower clusters are clipped off after blooming. You can deadhead up until early July; after that, you run the risk of cutting off next year's flower buds, which are on the two branches below the old flower cluster.

499 to rejuvenate an old lilac

An old, neglected lilac with tall, thick stems can be rejuvenated over a period of three years. Each year, cut one-third of the oldest branches back to the ground. Let a few new stems grow to replace them. After the third year, just cut back a few of the oldest branches each year, allowing new ones to grow in their place.

500 why lilacs don't bloom

Here's what to do if you lilacs fail to bloom:

- If they are less than five years old, do nothing. Lilacs won't bloom until they are three to five years old.
- Give the shrubs more light; prune overhanging tree branches or move the plants to a sunnier spot.
- Transplant them to a location with well-drained soil. They do not like dense, soggy soil.
- Cut back on nitrogen. If the leaves are big and lush, you may be overfeeding with nitrogen. Use a fertilizer high in phosphorus and potassium for a couple of years; then switch to a balanced formula. If the lilacs are in a lawn, keep lawn fertilizers away from them.

INDEX

158